Health Lesson 1

What is Health?

SonLight Education Ministry
United States of America

Copyright © 1995 by
SonLight Education Ministry
www.sonlighteducation.com

*You may use these materials for your immediate family,
classroom, or study group. No portion of this material
may be reproduced for profit, sold, or used for financial benefit.
This material belongs to SonLight Education Ministry
and is not to be distributed as the property
of any other person, ministry, or organization.*

A Suggested Daily Schedule

(Adapt this schedule to your family needs.)

5:00 a.m.		Arise–Personal Worship
6:00 a.m.		Family Worship and Bible Class–With Father
7:00 a.m.		Breakfast
8:00 a.m.		Practical Arts*–Domestic Activities 　　　　　　　Agriculture 　　　　　　　Industrial Arts 　　　　　　　(especially those related to 　　　　　　　the School Lessons)
10:00 a.m.		School Lessons (Take a break for some physical exercise during this time slot.)
12:00 p.m.		Dinner Preparations (Health class could be included at this time or a continued story.)
1:00 p.m.		Dinner
2:00 p.m.		Practical Arts* or Fine Arts (Music and Crafts) (especially those related to the School Lessons)
5:00 p.m.		Supper
6:00 p.m.		Family Worship–Father (Could do History Class)
7:00 p.m.		Personal time with God–Bed Preparation
8:00 p.m.		Bed

*Daily nature walk can be in morning or afternoon.

The Desire of All Nations

This book is a part of a curriculum that is built upon the life of Christ entitled, "The Desire of All Nations," for grades 2-8. Any of the books in this curriculum can be used by themselves or as an entire program.

INFORMATION ABOUT THE 2-8 GRADE PROGRAM

Multi-level

This program is written on a multi-level. That means that each booklet has material for grades 2-8. This is so the whole family in these grades may work from the same books. It is difficult for a busy mother to have 2 or more children and each have a different set of books. Remember, the Bible is written for all ages.

The Bible—the Primary Textbook

The books in this program are designed to teach the parent and the student how to learn academic subjects by using the Bible as a primary textbook.

The Desire of Ages

The Desire of Ages by Ellen G. White is used as a textbook to go with the Bible. This focuses on the early life of Christ, when He was a child. Children relate best to Christ as a child and youth.

Lesson Numbers

The big number in the top right corner on the cover of this book is the Lesson Number and corresponds with the chapter number in the book *The Desire of Ages*. For example, Lesson 1 in the school program will go along with chapter 1 in *The Desire of Ages*. Usually each family starts at the beginning with Lesson 1. Most children have not had a true Bible program, therefore they need the foundation built. If there is academic material that they have already covered, they do the Bible part and review then pass quickly on.

Seven Academic Subjects

There are seven academic subjects in this program—Health, Mathematics, Music, Science–Nature, History/Geography/Prophecy, Language, Voice–Speech.

Language Program

A good, solid language program is recommended to be used along with the SonLight materials.

The Riggs Institute has a multi-sensory teaching method that accommodates every child's unique learning style. Their program is called *Writing and Spelling Road to Reading and Thinking*. Order by calling (800) 200-4840 or visit www.riggsinst.org. (Disclaimer: SonLight does not endorse the reading books recommended in the Riggs' program.)

Another option which you might find more user friendly and is similar to the Riggs program but from a Christian perspective is *Spell to Write and Read* by Wanda Sanseri. To order, call Wanda Sanseri at (503) 654-2300 or visit https://www.bhibooks.net/swr.html

"God With Us"
Lesson 1 – Love

The following books are those you will need for this lesson.
All of these can be obtained from www.sonlighteducation.com

  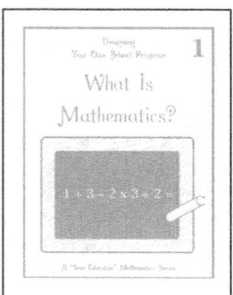  

The Rainbow Covenant – Study the spiritual meaning of colors and make your own rainbow book.

Health
What is Health?

Math
What is Mathematics?

Music
What is Music?

Science/Nature
What is Nature?

 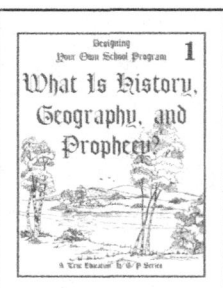   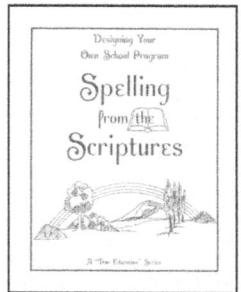

A Casket – Coloring book and story. Learn how to treat the gems of the Bible.

H/G/P
What is History, Geography and Prophecy?

Language
What is Language?

Speech/Voice
What is the Voice?

Spelling from the Scriptures

Bible Study – Learn how to study the Bible and helpful use tools.

Bible
The Desire of all Nations I
Teacher Study Guide
Student Study Guide
Bible Lesson Study Guide

Memory Verses
The Desire of all Nations I
Scripture Songs Book
and MP3 files

Our Nature Study Book – Your personal nature journal.

Outline of "The Desire of all Nations" Lesson 1

Bible	Health	Math	Music	Nature	H/G/P	Language	Voice

Week 1 Month 1
Lesson 1

Day 1

Family Morning Worship

Covenant Notebook
(1) Music, Prayer, MV
(2) Read pages 1-2 in the "Covenant Notebook" and discuss.
(3) Sometime during the day take a nature walk looking for rainbows.
(4) Begin finding pictures of complete rainbows to put into the plastic sheets behind the "Rainbows" page. Read and discuss the "Rainbows" page.

Use these songs during this week, "All Things Bright & Beautiful," "This is My Father's World," and "We Shall Know." Find this music in *Christ in Song* book which is included in these materials under the title "Song Books."

READ THIS BEFORE BEGINNING

Cover the Teacher's Section of each school book before beginning that subject.

It is best to cover only a few concepts at once and understand them well and not run a marathon with a young person's mind. If this outline moves to fast for you SLOW down. <u>Teach one idea and teach it well!</u>

This school program is not a race with time, rather it is an experience with God.

The parents are to represent their Father in Heaven before the children—students.

Together learn about the Character Qualities and help one another in a godly manner to reach the finish line together.

Day 2

(1) Music, Prayer, MV
(2) Read page 3 in the "Covenant Notebook" and discuss. (Also use page 7)

Lay out Lesson 1 of the School Program showing the front covers of each book, *What is Health?*, *What is Mathematics?*, *What is Music?*, *What is Nature?*, *What is H/G/P?*, *What is Language?*, and *What is Voice?*. Each book will have a color cover of one of the colors of the rainbow. Place them in order as the rainbow colors

deomonstrate in a picture. Refer to page 7 of the *Covenant Notebook* to see what each color means and how it relates to the subject that bears that color.

INSTRUCTIONS

(Examples: Health = Christ sacrificed His body on the cross for you.

Mathematics = Deals in numbers saved and lost.

Music = Right music can turn our thoughts from things of this world to Divinity.

Nature = Right growth in character.

H/G/P = The history of obedience and disobedience; geography of lands where the gospel is to be spread; prophecy telling us the future of those keeping the law.

Language and Voice = How God's royal people should write, speak, and act to prepare for His kingdom.

Bible	Health	Math	Music	Nature	H/G/P	Language	Voice
(3) Sometime during the day take a nature walk looking for rainbows. (4) Begin finding pictures of complete rainbows to put into the plastic sheets behind the "Rainbows" page. Read and discuss the "Rainbows" page. **Day 3-4** (1) Music, Prayer, MV (2) Read pages 4-9 in the "Covenant Notebook" and discuss. (3) Sometime during the day take a nature walk looking for white items (or the color pages). (4) Begin finding pictures of white things in nature to put into the plastic sheets behind the "White" page. Read and discuss the "White" page. **Day 5** Review what you have learned.							

INSTRUCTIONS

Once the white page is completed then move on to the red page and so forth, always finding things from nature for your pictures. And on your nature walks fine the color you are currently working on. Do not look for man made things! Before going on the nature walk each day, read and discuss the information in the color section.

After day 5, and reviewing only what you have learned to that point, plan only to work on the *Covenant Notebook* one day a week until that book is finished (Use time in the afternoon and not during the regular school hours). However, do not forget to review the *Covenant Notebook* when you deem it necessary, and if you should find a new picture for it, stop and put it into *Covenant Notebook*. It gives you an opportunity to review lessons with the children.

Lesson 12 of Nature in this series is about the rainbow and would be a wonderful time to make a recommitment to God.

This *Covenant Notebook* is to prepare you for the 2-8 School Lessons. On week 2 begin the School Lessons.

Bible	Health	Math	Music	Nature	H/G/P	Language	Voice
Week 2 Lesson 1		START THE 2-8 PROGRAM, "The Desire Of All Nations."					
Day 1 "God With Us" (1) Music ("O Come, O come, Immanuel," "I Love Thee," "Thou didst Leave Thy Throne"), Prayer, MV (Mt 1:21) (2) Read and discuss Ge 3:14-15; 12:1-3. Discuss the Character Quality.	**Day 1** *What Is Health?* (1) Open Bibles and read II Sa 20:9. (2) Read or tell information. Do pages 1-17 or what you can cover. Discuss.	**Day 1** *What Is Math...?* (1) Open Bibles and read Mt 11:29. (2) Read or tell information. Do pages 1-8 or what you can cover. Discuss.				**Day 1** *Writing and Spelling Road to Reading and Thinking (WSRRT)* (1) Do your daily assignments for *WSRRT*. If you are still working on this program continue until you finish at least the 2nd teacher's notebook.	

INSTRUCTIONS

If you are still using the *Family Bible Lessons* do them for one of your worships each day and use *The Desire of all Nations* for the other worship each day.

These are the items you will need for worship for *The Desire of all Nations* Bible program: Old King James Bible (**NOT** the New King James Bible)
  "*The Desire of all Nations,*" Volume 1, Study Guide for the KJV Bible Lessons
  The Desire of all Nations Teacher and Student Study Guides #1 (Chapters from *The Desire of Ages* Bible text book)
  The Desire of all Nations Song Book #1 and CD Music #1 for Memory Verses
  Christ in Song Song Book #1, 2, 3, 4

These are the items you will need for class time:

  What is Health?; What is Mathematics; What is Music?; What is Nature?; What is H/G/P?; What is Language?; and What is Voice?.
  Our Nature Study Book   "The Casket" Story & Coloring Book
  Bible Study
  Road Map and Route Catalogue

vii

Bible	Health	Math	Music	Nature	H/G/P	Language	Voice
Day 2 "God With Us" (1) Music ("O Come, O come, Immanuel," "I Love Thee," "Thou didst Leave Thy Throne"), Prayer, MV (Mt 1:21; Jn 8:28) (2) Read and discuss Gal 3:16; Ge 49:10; De 18:17-19; II Sam 7:12-17.	**Day 2** *What Is Health?* (1) Open Bibles and read I Co 12:23. (2) Read or tell information. Do pages 18-26 or what you can cover. Discuss.	**Day 2** *What Is Math...?* (1) Open Bibles and read Luke 6:38; Is 40:12; Ps 147:4; Is 40:26; Job 28:25. (2) Read or tell information. Do pages 9-22 or what you can cover. Discuss. **END**				**Day 2** *Writing and Spelling Road to Reading and Thinking* (1) Do your daily assignments for *WSRRT*.	
Day 3 "God With Us" (1) Music, Prayer, MV (Mt 1:21; Jn 8:28) (2) Read and discuss Ez 21:25-27; Lu 1:32; Isa 9:6-7.	**Day 3** *What Is Health?* (1) Open Bibles and read Pr 26:2. (2) Read or tell information. Do pages 27-35 or what you can cover. Discuss.		**Day 3** *What Is Music?* (1) Open Bibles and read Zeph 3:17. (2) Read or tell information. Do pages 1-6 or what you can cover. Discuss.				
Day 4 "God With Us" (1) Review what you have already covered.	**Day 4** *What Is Health?* (1) Review pages 1-35.	**Day 4** *What Is Math...?* (1) Review.	**Day 4** *What Is Music?* (1) Open Bibles and read Re 14:2-3. (2) Read or tell information. Do pages 7-17 or what you can cover. Discuss.			**Day 4** *Writing and Spelling Road to Reading and Thinking* (1) Do your daily assignments for *WSRRT*.	
Day 5	**Day 5**	**Day 5**	**Day 5**			**Day 5** Review	

Find practical applications from your textbooks you have thus far used this week. You will find them listed under "**Reinforce.**" Choose and use today.

Bible	Health	Math	Music	Nature	H/G/P	Language	Voice
Week 3 Lesson 1							
Day 1 "God With Us" (1) Music, Prayer, MV (Mt 1:21; Jn 8:28) (2) Read and discuss Ps 45:1-8; 72:1-11; Is 53.	**Day 1** *What Is Health?* (1) Open Bibles and read James 5:14. (2) Read or tell information. Do pages 36-39 or what you can cover. Discuss.		**Day 1** *What Is Music?* (1) Open Bibles and read I Ki 19:12. (2) Read or tell information. Do pages 18-30 or what you can cover. Discuss.			**Day 1** *Writing and Spelling Road to Reading and Thinking* (1) Do your daily assignments for *WSRRT*.	
Day 2 "God With Us" (1) Music, Prayer, MV (Mt 1:21; Jn 8:28; Jn 8:50) (2) Read and discuss Zec 12:10; Jn 14:9; Mt 1:23; Jn 1:1-4.	**Day 2** *What Is Health?* (1) Open Bibles and read De 34:7. (2) Read or tell information. Do pages 40-44 or what you can cover. Discuss.		**Day 2** *What Is Music?* (1) Open Bibles and read I Chr 13:8. (2) Read or tell information. Do pages 31-52 or what you can cover. Discuss. END			**Day 2** *Writing and Spelling Road to Reading and Thinking* (1) Do your daily assignments for *WSRRT*.	
Day 3 "God With Us" (1) Music, Prayer, MV (Mt 1:21; Jn 8:28; Jn 8:50; Phil 2:5-11) (2) Read and discuss *The Desire of Ages* 19-20:0.	**Day 3** *What Is Health?* (1) Open Bibles and read Ez 33:11. (2) Read or tell information. Do pages 45-53 or what you can cover. Discuss.			**Day 3** *What Is Nature?* (1) Open Bibles and read Ro 13:10. (2) Read or tell information. Do pages 1-11 or what you can cover. Discuss.		**Day 3** *Writing and Spelling Road to Reading and Thinking* (1) Do your daily assignments for *WSRRT*.	

Bible	Health	Math	Music	Nature	H/G/P	Language	Voice
Day 4 "God With Us" (1) Music, Prayer, MV (Mt 1:21; Jn 8:28; Jn 8:50; Phil 2:5-11) (2) Read and discuss *The Desire of Ages* 20:2-21:0.	**Day 4** *What Is Health?* (1) Open Bibles and read De 7:15; De 32:46; and Pr 4:20, 22. (2) Read or tell information. Do pages 54-60 or what you can cover. Discuss.			**Day 4** *What Is Nature?* (1) Open Bibles and read Ps 40:5; Ps 111:4. (2) Read or tell information. Do pages 12-17 or what you can cover. Discuss.		**Day 4** *Writing and Spelling Road to Reading and Thinking* (1) Do your daily assignments for *WSRRT*.	
Day 5 "God With Us" (1) Review.	**Day 5** *What Is Health?* (1) Review pages 1-60.	**Day 5** *What Is Math...?* (1) Review.	**Day 5** *What Is Music?* (1) Review.	**Day 5** *What Is Nature?* (1) Review pages 1-17.		**Day 5** *Writing and Spelling Road to Reading and Thinking* (1) Do your daily assignments for *WSRRT*.	
Week 4 Lesson 1 **Day 1** "God With Us" (1) Music, Prayer, MV (Mt 1:21; Jn 8:28; Jn 8:50; Phil 2:5-11) (2) Read and discuss *The Desire of Ages* 21:1-2.	**Day 1** *What Is Health?* (1) Open Bibles and read De 7:15; De 32:46; and Pr 4:20, 22. (2) Read the story. Do pages 61-80. Discuss.			**Day 1** *What Is Nature?* (1) Open Bibles and read Job 12:7-8. (2) Read or tell information. Do pages 18-23 or what you can cover. Discuss.		**Day 1** *Writing and Spelling Road to Reading and Thinking* (1) Do your daily assignments for *WSRRT*.	
Day 2 "God With Us" (1) Music, Prayer, MV (Mt 1:21; Jn 8:28; Jn 8:50; Phil 2:5-11) (2) Read and discuss *The Desire of Ages* 21:3-22:1.	**Day 2** *What Is Health* (1) Open Bibles and review De 7:15; De 32:46; and Pr 4:20, 22. (2) Do pages 81-86. Discuss. **END**			**Day 2** *What Is Nature?* (1) Open Bibles and read Ps 143:5. (2) Read or tell information. Do pages 24-30 or what you can cover. **END**		**Day 2** *WSRRT* (1) Do your daily assignments for *WSRRT*. Continue the *WSRRT* but add the Language lessons in whenever it is time to do them. **This will not be repeated.**	

Bible	Health	Math	Music	Nature	H/G/P	Language	Voice
Day 3 "God With Us" (1) Music, Prayer, MV (Mt 1:21; Jn 8:28; Jn 8:50; Phil 2:5-11) (2) Read and discuss *The Desire of Ages* 21:3-22:3.					**Day 3** *What Is H/G/P?* (1) Open Bibles and read He 1:10. (2) Read or tell information. Do pages 1-6 or what you can cover. Discuss. Choose a good mission book to begin reading as a family.	**Day 3** *What Is Language?* (1) Open Bibles and read Col 3:16. (2) Read or tell information. Do pages 1-10 or what you can cover + *WSRRT*. Discuss.	
Day 4 "God With Us" (1) Music, Prayer, MV (Mt 1:21; Jn 8:28; Jn 8:50; Phil 2:5-11) (2) Read and discuss *The Desire of Ages* 21:3-22:3.					**Day 4** *What Is H/G/P?* (1) Open Bibles and read Ps 119:105 & He 13:1. (2) Read or tell information. Do pages 7-14. Discuss.	**Day 4** *What Is Language?* (1) Open Bibles and read Pr 25:11. (2) Read or tell information. Do pages 11-17 + *WSRRT*. Discuss.	**Day 4** *What Is Voice?* (1) Open Bibles and read Ps 105:2. (2) Read or tell information. Do pages 1-4. Discuss.
Day 5 "God With Us" (1) Review. (2) Read and discuss *The Desire of Ages* 22:4-24:1.	**Day 5** *What Is Health?* (1) Review	**Day 5** *What Is Math...?* (1) Review.	**Day 5** *What Is Music?* (1) Review.	**Day 5** *What Is Nature?* (1) Review.	**Day 5** *What Is H/G/P?* (1) Review pages 1-14.	**Day 5** *What Is Language?* (1) Review pages 1-17.	**Day 5** *What Is Voice?* (1) Review pages 1-4.
Week 1 (5) Lesson 1 **Month 2**		If there is any information that the student should know and does not—REVIEW.				Do your daily assignments for *WSRRT*.	
Day 1 "God With Us" (1) Music, Prayer, MV (Mt 1:21; Jn 8:28; Jn 8:50; Phil 2:5-11) (2) Read and discuss *The Desire of Ages* 24:2-26:3.					**Day 1** *What Is H/G/P?* (1) Open Bibles and read Jer 10:12. (2) Read or tell information. Do pages 15-25Aa or what you can cover. Discuss.	**Day 1** *What Is Language?* (1) Open Bibles and read Jn 1:1. (2) Read or tell information. Do pages 18-22 or what you can cover. Discuss. **END**	**Day 1** *What Is Voice?* (1) Open Bibles and read Ps 32:2. (2) Read or tell information. Do pages 5-8. Discuss. **END**

Bible	Health	Math	Music	Nature	H/G/P	Language	Voice
Day 2 "God With Us" (1) Music, Prayer, MV. (2) Expand or review any part of the lesson. (Could use section about William Miller in H/G/P.)					**Day 2** *What Is H/G/P?* (1) Open Bibles and read II Pe 1:21. (2) Read or tell information. Do pages 26-47 or what you can cover. Discuss. (Story about "William Miller" may take longer.)	**Day 2** *Writing and Spelling Road to Reading and Thinking* (1) Do your daily assignments for *WSRRT*.	**Day 2** *What Is Voice?* (1) Review
Day 3 "God With Us" (1) Music, Prayer, MV. (2) Expand or review any part of the lesson. (Could use the section in II/G/P, "The Schools of the Prophets.")					**Day 3** *What Is H/G/P?* (1) Open Bibles and read Ja 3:17 & Pr 9:10. (2) Read or tell information. Do pages 48-65 or what you can cover. Discuss.	**Day 3** *Writing and Spelling Road to Reading and Thinking* (1) Do your daily assignments for *WSRRT*.	
Day 4 "God With Us" (1) Music, Prayer, MV. (2) Expand or review any part of the lesson. (Could explain why the Apocrypha books are not included in Bible.) **END**					**Day 4** *What Is H/G/P?* (1) Open Bibles and read Ex 17:14 & Ge 5:22. (2) Read or tell information. Do pages 66-78 or what you can cover. Discuss. **END**	**Day 4** *Writing and Spelling Road to Reading and Thinking* (1) Do your daily assignments for *WSRRT*.	**Day 4-5** Use this time to review anything from lesson 1.
		On day 5 review any subject in Lesson 1 that needs a better understanding.					
Week 2 **Month 2** **Lesson 2** **Day 1** "The Chosen People" (1) Music, Prayer, MV. (2) Read and discuss.		Continue the process with Lesson 2. See the *Road Map and Route Catalogue*.					

Health Instructions

1. For **Place I** in Health class have the child lie down on a large piece of paper and draw his outline. Then, as he draws body parts in each lesson he can cut them out, and paste them on the outline of his body in the correct place.

2. When teaching prevention of disease or natural treatments have the child do any treatments possible so he will become familiar with giving them.

3. You will need a medical dictionary for older students to define their spelling words.

4. Sharing the lessons learned is important. Have small cooking classes or preventative life-style meetings with one or two willing friends for your children to present what they have learned in class.

5. Remember, to make parallels with the Bible lessons.

Table of Contents

Teachers Section   **Pages 1-18**

Student Section   **Pages 1-87**

Research

Health	Page 1
Lack of Knowledge	Page 2
Health Is....	Page 3
Law of **Love**	Page 3
"Health is Wealth" – Poem	Page 4
Health Questionnaire	Page 5
The Importance of Good Health	Page 7
Health and Talents	Page 8
The Birthright Blessing	Page 8
Ten Commandments of Health	Page 10
The "New Commandment"	Page 13
Guard It	Page 14
Reflect – "Our Greatest Wealth" – Poem	Page 14
Review	Page 15

Research

Actions of the Organs	Page 18
Remedying a Problem	Page 19
Reinforce – "Quiz"	Page 19
Review	Page 20
Remind	Page 21
Reflect	Page 21
"Sunlight in the Heart" – Sing This Song	Page 22
"Every Attention but One" – Story	Page 24

Research

Causes	Page 27
Drugs and Disease	Page 28
Nature's Effort	Page 28
Natural Remedies	Page 29
Reflect	Page 29
Review	Page 30

"Our Eight Natural Doctors" – Poem	Page 31
Do You Know the Secret to Good Health?	Page 32
Review	Page 33
"The Praise of Good Doctors" – Poem	Page 35

Research

Sickness and Disease	Page 36
Review	Page 37
Remind	Page 39

Research

Vital Capital	Page 40
Reflect	Page 42
"Accounted For" – Poem	Page 43
Review	Page 44

Research

The Point of No Return	Page 45
Harken	Page 46
"Lifespan Chart" – Illustration	Page 48
Vitality Summary	Page 50
Remind	Page 50
Review	Page 51
"A Sound Mind in a Sound Body" – Poem	Page 52

Research

Conditions of Cure	Page 54
Reinforce	Page 55
The Goal	Page 55
Grace is Needed	Page 56
Reinforce	Page 56
"The Great Physician" – Sing This Song	Page 57
Reinforce	Page 58
"Physical Healing" – Bible Search	Page 60
Reinforce	Page 60
"Some Chapters of Bob's Early Life" – Story	Page 61
Review	Page 79
"Gertrude's Graveyard" – Story	Page 81
"Health" – Mark Your Bible	Page 85

Teacher Section

*"Behold,
I will bring it
health and cure,
and I will cure them,
and will reveal unto them
the abundance of peace and truth."*
Jeremiah 33:6

*"That thy way
may be known upon earth,
thy saving health among all nations."*
Psalm 67:2

INSTRUCTIONS
For the Teacher

Step 1

Study the Bible lesson and begin to memorize the memory verses. Familiarize yourself with the character quality.

The student can answer the Bible review questions. See page 5. Use the steps in Bible study.

Bible Lesson

"God With Us" – Genesis 3:14-15; 12:1-3; Galatians 3:16; Genesis 49:10; Deuteronomy 18:17-19; II Samuel 7:12-17; Ezekiel 21:25-27; Luke 1:32; Isaiah 9:6-7; Psalm 45:1-8; 72:1-11; Isaiah 53; Zechariah 12:10; John 14:9; John 1:1-4; Matthew 1:23

Memory Verses

Matthew 1:20-21; 1:23; John 8:28; 6:57; 7:18; 8:50; Philippians 2:5-11

Character Quality

Love – an affection of the mind excited by beauty and worth of any kind, or by the qualities of an object; charity.

Antonyms – hate; detestableness; abomination; loathing; scorn; disdainfulness; selfishness

Character Quality Verse

I Corinthians 13:4-7 – *"Charity suffereth long, and is kind; charity envieth not; charity vaunteth not itself, is not puffed up,*

"Doth not behave itself unseemly, seeketh not her own, is not easily provoked, thinketh no evil;

"Rejoiceth not in iniquity, but rejoiceth in the truth;

"Beareth all things, believeth all things, hopeth all things, endureth all things."

Step 2

Understand How To/ And

A. Do the spelling cards so the student can begin to build his own spiritual dictionary.

What is Health? - Teacher - Page 1

B. Mark the Bible.

C. Evaluate your student's character in relation to the character quality of **love**.

D. Familiarize yourself with the human body. Notice the projects.

E. Review the Scripture references for "Health."

F. Notice the Answer Key.

A. Spelling Cards
Spelling Lists

Health Words
Place I - II - III

absence	enmity
action	forever
balanced	head
body	heel
cleansing	Judah
disease	kingdom
health	lawgiver
love	peace
nutritive	Prophet
sickness	scepter
	seed
Bible Words	Shiloh
blessing	throne
bruise	woman
Emmanuel	

See the booklet
Spelling from the Scriptures
for instructions about how to make the Spelling Cards.

B. How to Mark the Bible

1. Copy the list of Bible texts in the back of the Bible on an empty page as a guide.

2. Go to the first text in the Bible and copy the next text beside it. Go to the next one and repeat the process until they are all chain referenced.

3. Have the student present the study to family and/or friends.

4. Each student lesson has one or more sections that have a Bible marking study on the subject studied. (See the student's section, pages 60 and 85.)

C. Evaluate Your Student's Character

This section is for the purpose of helping the teacher know how to encourage the students to become more **loving**.

See page 7.

Place I = Grades 2-3-4
Place II = Grades 4-5-6
Place III = Grades 6-7-8

What is Health? - Teacher - Page 2

D. Familiarize Yourself With the Health of the Body – Notice the Projects

Projects

1. As a family, choose several ways to improve your health and work on these for a year (example: more exercise).

2. Find the 8 laws of health demonstrated in the animal kingdom (nutrition, exercise, water, sunlight, temperance, fresh air, rest, trust in God). (Example: some birds go to their rest early each evening.)

3. Be like the body organs and assist others. Choose someone in your family, neighborhood, or church and see if there is something you can do to aid them. Perhaps you could gather firewood or rake the lawn for a widow. *"Strengthen ye the weak hands, and confirm the feeble knees"* (Isaiah 35:3).

4. As a family, discuss this question: "Do you know the difference between the health of Heaven and the health of Earth?"

5. Memorize Bible verses concerning health.

6. As a family, attend a nutrition seminar. If there is not one available in your area, rent a DVD series about nutrition.

7. Study more about the Levitical health code from the Bible.

8. Learn to make homemade bread.

9. Learn to sing the song, "Love at Home," found at the end of the Teacher's Section.

What is Health? - Teacher - Page 3

E. Review the Scripture References for "Health"

Teacher, read through this section before working on the lesson with the student.

See page 8.

F. Notice the Answer Key

The answer key for the student book is found on page 9.

Step 3

Read the Lesson Aim.

Lesson Aim

This lesson is to be an introduction to Health. It is to teach the child the character quality of **love** through "God With Us."

God sent His Son Jesus to this world as the unwearied servant of man's necessity. He *"took our infirmities, and bare our sicknesses,"* that He might minister to the needs of humanity (Matthew 8:17). It was His mission to restore man to health. He came also to give peace and perfection of character.

Jesus came in **love** to heal us physically, mentally, and spiritually. Health teaches us about our bodies, how they work, and how to cooperate with God so they can work the very best. If we **love** Him, we will want to cooperate with Him.

As we study the body we will see the Creator's law of self-sacrificing **love** working among its members. When the body is healthy, each organ *"seeketh not her own,"* but works to benefit the other organs (I Corinthians 13:5). Also, in disease, each organ bears the infirmities of the weaker organs and works extra hard to make up for any lack caused by injured or sick members. This illustrates the **love** we should have for each other as members of the body of Christ. *"We then that are strong ought to bear the infirmities of the weak, and not to please ourselves. Let everyone of us please his neighbor for his good to edification. For even Christ pleased not Himself; but as it is written, The reproaches of them that reproached thee fell on me"* (Romans 15:1-3).

Step 4

Prepare to begin the Health Lesson.

To Begin the Health Lesson

One way to introduce the lesson might be to take the child to a place where he can see someone very ill with a disease.

Step 5

Begin the Health lesson. Cover only what can be understood by your student. Make the lessons a family project by involving the whole family in part or all of the lesson. These lessons are designed for the whole family.

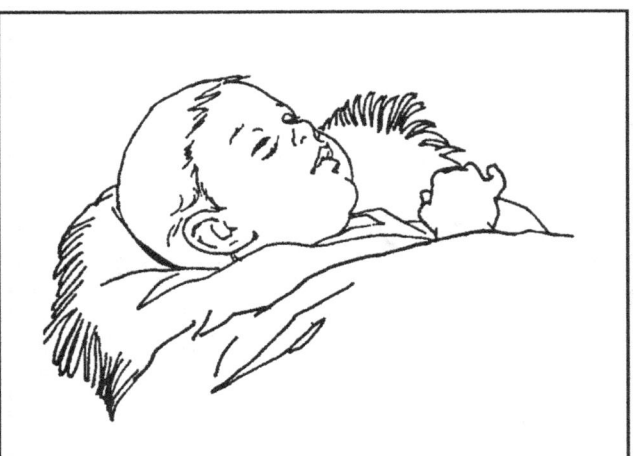

Steps in Bible Study

1. Prayer

2. Read the verses/meditate/memorize.

3. Look up key words in *Strong's Concordance* and find their meanings in the Hebrew or Greek dictionary in the back of that book.

4. Cross reference (marginal reference) with other Bible texts. An excellent study tool is *The Treasury of Scripture Knowledge*.

5. Use Bible custom books for more information on the times.

6. Write a summary of what you have learned from those verses.

7. Mark key thoughts in the margin of your Bible.

8. Share your study with others to reinforce the lessons you have learned.

What is Health? - Teacher - Page 5

Review Questions

1. What were the circumstances under which the first promise of a Redeemer was given? (Genesis 3:14-15)

2. What promise was made to Abraham, and what did it mean? (Genesis 12:1-3; Galatians 3:16)

3. Through what tribe of Israel was the Messiah to come? (Genesis 49:10)

4. What promise was given through Moses? (Deuteronomy 18:17-19)

5. Through whom was the permanence of David's kingdom assured? (II Samuel 7:12-17; Ezekiel 21:25-27; Luke 1:32-33)

6. What exalted ideas concerning the Messiah were made prominent? (Isaiah 9:6, 7; Psalm 45:1-8; 72:1-11)

7. What also was foretold of His relation to sin? (Isaiah 53; Zechariah 12:10)

8. What is the significance of the name which John applies to Christ? (Matthew 1:23; John 14:9)

9. What important facts are stated of Him in John 1:1-4
   a.
   b.
   c.

10. As part of the great scheme of human redemption, what did the Word become? What is the meaning of the words *"became flesh?"* (Matthew 1:23)

Notes

What is Health? - Teacher - Page 6

Evaluating Your Child's Character

Check the appropriate box for your student's level of development,
or your own, as the case may be.

Maturing Nicely (MN), Needs Improvement (NI), Poorly Developed (PD), Absent (A)

Love

1. *"Charity suffereth long and is kind"* (I Corinthians 13:4). Does the child show a maturity of **love** that enables him to be kind while suffering from hunger, tiredness, or discomfort?

   MN   NI   PD   A
   ❏   ❏   ❏   ❏

2. When the child encounters people with character deficiencies, is the child's reaction one of **loving** pity and concern instead of condemnation?

   MN   NI   PD   A
   ❏   ❏   ❏   ❏

3. Does the child seem to **love** God more as a result of studying the material contained in the Bible?

   MN   NI   PD   A
   ❏   ❏   ❏   ❏

4. *"Charity...vaunteth not itself; is not puffed up."* Does the child refrain from comparing himself with others? Does he make comments like "I can read better than _____ ."

   MN   NI   PD   A
   ❏   ❏   ❏   ❏

5. *"Charity...seeketh not her own."* Is the child willing for others to have the best or the most of desirable things?

   MN   NI   PD   A
   ❏   ❏   ❏   ❏

6. *"Love your enemies."* Does the child initiate reconciliation with or do kind things for those who have hard feelings toward him or who have treated him unfairly?

   MN   NI   PD   A
   ❏   ❏   ❏   ❏

7. *"Love covers a multitude of sins."* Is the child eager to tell you about the failures of others or does he **lovingly** shield others from exposure where possible to do so with integrity?

   MN   NI   PD   A
   ❏   ❏   ❏   ❏

8. *"Charity...thinketh no evil."* Is the child unsuspecting, ever placing the most favorable construction upon the motives and acts of others?

   MN   NI   PD   A
   ❏   ❏   ❏   ❏

What is Health? - Teacher - Page 7

Scripture References
"Health"

III John 2 – *"Beloved, I wish above all things that thou mayest prosper and be in health, even as thy soul prospereth."*

Proverbs 4:20-23 – *"My son, attend to my words; incline thine ear unto my sayings. Let them not depart from thine eyes; keep them in the midst of thine heart. For they are life unto those that find them, and health to all their flesh. Keep thy heart with all diligence; for out of it are the issues of life."*

Psalm 67:2 – *"That thy way may be known upon earth, thy saving health among all nations."*

Proverbs 3:7-8 – *"Be not wise in thine own eyes: fear the Lord, and depart from evil. It shall be health to thy navel, and marrow to thy bones."*

Proverbs 12:18 – *"...the tongue of the wise is health."*

Proverbs 16:24 – *"Pleasant words are as an honeycomb, sweet to the soul, and health to the bones."*

Isaiah 58:8 – *"Then shall thy light break forth as the morning, and thine health shall spring forth speedily: and thy righteousness shall go before thee."*

Jeremiah 30:17 – *"For I will restore health unto thee, and I will heal thee of thy wounds, saith the Lord."*

Jeremiah 33:6 – *"Behold, I will bring it health and cure, and I will cure them, and will reveal unto them the abundance of peace and truth."*

Psalm 42:11 – *"Why art thou cast down, O my soul? and why art thou disquieted within me? hope thou in God: for I shall yet praise him, who is the health of my countenance, and my God."*

Psalm 119:93 – *"I will never forget thy precepts: for with them thou hast quickened me."*

Proverbs 10:27 – *"The fear of the Lord prolongeth days: but the years of the wicked shall be shortened."*

Answer Key

Page 15

1. Teacher, check.

2. body, mind, duties, pain

3. sum, normally

4. Health, God wants to restore man completely. *"I pray God your whole spirit and soul and body be preserved blameless unto the coming of our Lord Jesus Christ"* (I Thessalonians 5:23).

Page 16

5. All should be circled.

6. labor, life, health

7. See page 2 of Teacher's Section.

8. A. - O
   B. - O
   C. - O
   D. - O
   E. - O

Page 17

   F. - O
   G. - O

Page 17 continued

9. See page 2 of the Student's Section.

10. Student answers. (We are only managers, not owners of our body temples under God.)

11. Character

12. III John 2

13. Not to sin again lest a worse thing come upon them.

14. obedience

15. health, mind

16. See page 7 of the Student's Section. (All true happiness is made up of right feeling. The perfect conditions of right feelings are the vigorous, healthful exercise of all the mental powers, combined with the normal action of the bodily functions. Therefore, the highest kind of happiness comes from the combination of a healthy body plus a healthy mind. If we strictly followed the laws of our being, comfort and satisfaction would flow within us.

17. Student answers.

What is Health? - Teacher - Page 9

Answer Key

Page 19

Left to right top row of organs: heart, pelvic bones, brain, eye, spleen

Bottom row of organs: liver, ear, lung, shoulder muscles, voice box, kidney

Page 20

1. breaking one of the laws of health

2. some other organ takes on the extra work

3. taking on the extra work of other organs

4. harmonious, pleasant feeling, energy

5. energy, getting sick

6. It implies that the body needs energy or strength in order to resist or overcome disease. A lack of energy should be a warning that we are susceptible to disease and that something is out of balance in the system.

7. nutritive actions
   cleansing actions

Page 20 continued

8. when the nutritive and cleansing actions get out of balance

9. The nutritive actions would outweigh the body's ability to purify itself. Or the organs could be strained by having too much work to do in dealing with the unneeded nutrition.

Page 27

1. B.
2. C.
3. D.
4. A.
5. B.

Page 30

1. sunlight
2. water
3. rest
4. proper diet
5. pure air
6. exercise
7. temperance
8. trust in God

Page 33

1. pure blood, perfect circulation
   impure blood, circulation

What is Health? - Teacher - Page 10

Answer Key

Page 33 continued

2. Student answers. Example:
I John 1:7 says *"the blood of Jesus Christ his Son cleanseth us from all sin."* The blood cleanses and builds up the tissues and Christ's sacrifice nourishes and cleanses us spiritually. To be spiritually perfected and sanctified Christ's blood must cleanse the entire life, just as the circulation needs to be perfect in order to have perfect health. The love of Christ must flow through us. David said *"purge me with hyssop (an herb used to purify the blood), and I shall be clean; wash me* (in Jesus' blood), *and I shall be whiter than snow* (spiritual cleanliness)" (Psalm 51:7).

Page 34

1. G.
2. H.
3. B.
4. A.
5. D.
6. E.
7. F.
8. C.

Page 36

Sickness = ill health; illness

Page 36 continued

Disease = To interrupt or impair any or all the natural and regular functions of the various organs of a living body

Page 37

1. Teacher, check. (Psalm 107:17)

Page 38

2. b. and c.

3. Cough – c.
   Fever – a.
   Sneeze – f.
   Painful redness and swelling – d.
   Chills – e.
   Pimples – b.

4. See page 36 of the Student's Section.

Page 40

force – freshness, vigor, natural force
abated – flit, vanished away

Page 51

1. reserved, force, emergencies

What is Health? - Teacher - Page 11

Answer Key

Page 51 continued

2. to be kept in store for future or special use

3. natural force

4. yes

5. Because at first there are no serious ill effects to transgressing natural law. The reserve force equals the demand. But by and by the body is drained of its reserve force and cannot recover its balance so easily. Then people are surprised at the serious consequences that follow seemingly small habitual transgressions.

6. Carefully save what force is left and build up the health by strictly complying with all the laws of health. Pray for God's grace. *"He restoreth my soul"* (Psalm 23:3).

7. Little transgressions can lead to chronic diseases by exhausting the vital capital and keeping the body from repairing or cleansing itself.

8. God's way of curing disease is to build up health. A healthy body results in a mind that is clearer and more sensitive to receiving instruction from God.

9. If a person continues to transgress the laws of health he will have less and less vital capital and so he will become subject to worse or more serious or chronic diseases.

Page 58

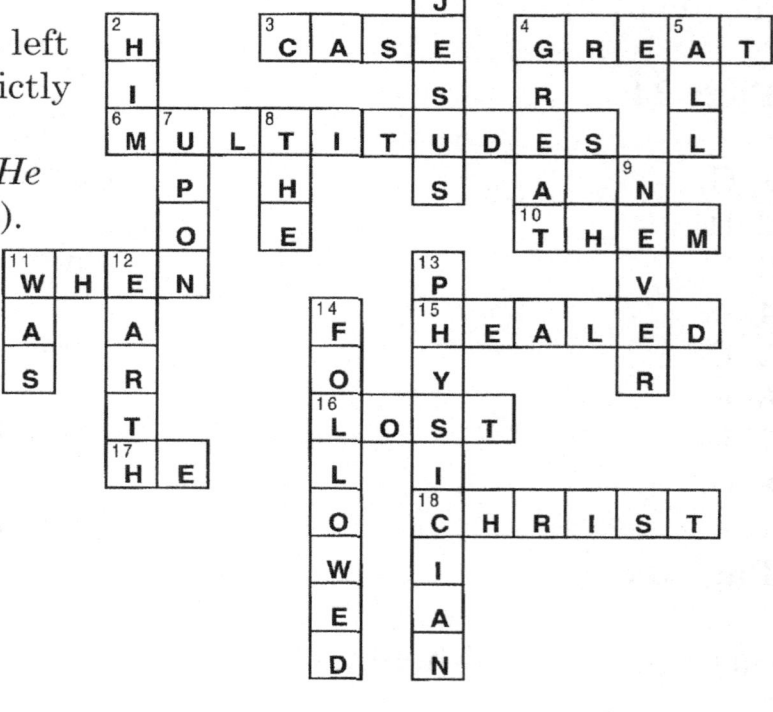

What is Health? - Teacher - Page 12

Answer Key

Page 60

1. prayer

2. dip 7 times in the River Jordan

3. prayer of faith, effectual fervent prayer of a righteous man

4. Hezekiah, lump of figs over a boil

5. God's word

6. Memorize Psalm 41:1-4

7. sick head, faint heart, wounds, bruises, and putrefying sores

8. Trophimus, Epaphroditus

Page 79

1. Teacher, check. Some ideas are: The abstinence movement and temperance meetings; the intemperate desire of the boys to be able to eat as many sweets as they liked; proper clothing and proper diet was lacking in the prison, there was also insufficient covers for the beds, etc.

2. It was cold in the winter and hot in the summer and only had one tiny window to let in light and fresh air.

Page 79 continued

3. He lost his toes as a result of frostbite in the prison. His mother got sick with a fever from the stress and grief of learning about Bob's crime.

4. Ned did not have a mother to **love** and care for him, or to **lovingly** tell him what was good or bad.

5. sweets, or the pleasures of this world

6. The 8th commandment, *"Thou shalt not steal"* (Exodus 20:15).

7. It seems as though he was inclined to eat more than is healthful.

"Let your moderation be known unto all men" (Philippians 4:5).

8. It caused her anxiety, grief, sleeplessness and because of her concern she took no food nor warmed her apartment in cold weather. Her body became weakened as a result and she developed a fever.

9. It was cold; the bed-covers were thin; the food was poor.

What is Health? - Teacher - Page 13

Answer Key

Page 79 continued

10. His body was more delicate or fragile. He was weaker and less able to endure the cold.

11. Pain made him walk carefully and this would in itself help him to avoid further injury to them. Pain is a **loving** warning signal the body gives when some part is injured or sick.

12. shoes

13. Mr. and Mrs. Greenwood
They took him into their own home until his mother got out of the hospital.

14. It lessened her strength so that she was not able to do as much as before.

15. Bob lost his toes due to unhealthy living conditions in prison and people would not hire him because his missing toes testified that he had been a criminal and they were afraid to trust him. Bell's loss of health and weakened condition made her unable to perform the same amount of work she used to.

16. connection

Page 79 continued

17. He put it into the hearts of some people to give them coal and food.

18. Church members who held temperance and church services for their area showed **love** for their community. They showed their personal concern for others by going house-to-house and inviting the people personally to the first meeting.

19. when going house-to-house

Page 80

20. The wicked storekeeper who bought the stolen brass fittings from Ned and Bob broke the law which says, *"thou shalt **love** thy neighbor as thyself"* (Leviticus 19:18). He was not obeying the golden rule. He would not have wanted someone to knowingly buy stolen goods from his own shop.

21. Mr. Greenwood supplied him a new suit of clothes which would not have to be paid for until Bob got rich. The shoemaker gave him a pair of shoes on the same terms.

What is Health? - Teacher - Page 14

Answer Key

Page 80 continued

22. He paid for a better place for her to live. He supplied her every comfort and was very attentive to her. He wrote her weekly and took her on trips.

23. **love** for his mother

Love At Home

There is beauty all around,
When there's **love** at home;
There is joy in ev'ry sound,
When there's **love** at home.
Peace and plenty here abide,
Smiling fair on ev'ry side;
Time doth softly, sweetly glide,
When there's **love** at home.

♡ Brotherly *Love*

*" 'By this shall all men know
that ye are my disciples,
if ye have **love** one to another.'
The more closely we resemble
our Saviour in character,
the greater will be our **love**
toward those for whom He died.
Christians who manifest a spirit
of unselfish **love** for one another
are bearing a testimony for Christ
which unbelievers
can neither gainsay nor resist.
It is impossible to estimate the power
of such an example. Nothing will
so successfully defeat the devices of Satan
and his emissaries, nothing will so build
up the Redeemer's kingdom,
as will the **love** of Christ manifested
by the members of the church.
Peace and prosperity can be enjoyed
only as meekness and **love**
are in active exercise."*

5 Testimonies 167-168

What is Health? - Teacher - Page 18

Gardening Sheet

Lesson __One__ Subject __Health__

Title __"What is Health"__

In Season	Out of Season
We know God **loves** us for it is written: *"Beloved, I wish above all things that thou mayest prosper and be in health, even as thy soul prospereth"* (III John 2). As you plan your gardens (flowers or vegetables) lawns, shrubs and trees plan to plant them were they will get all they need to be <u>healthy</u>. They need sunshine, water, and fertilizer. There needs to be sufficient space for each plant to grow. The plants can also be attractively arranged in the garden, orchard or around the house. When we are in good health we will have a glow about us and be attractive. Draw out a sketch of flower beds, orchard, and vegetable garden. Consider companion planting. (That means two varieties of plants by each other to assist in keeping the insect pests away.) Gather gardening books to find ideas about lay-out and planning. Learn more about gardening this year as you learn more about health.	<u>Planning</u> flower beds, orchards, and vegetable gardens can be a winter activity. The library has many good books about gardening.

Student Section

*"For I will restore health
unto thee,
and I will heal thee
of thy wounds,
saith the Lord."*
Jeremiah 30:17

*"...Present your bodies
a living sacrifice..."*
Romans 12:1

WHAT IS HEALTH?

Research
Health

"...Art thou in health, my brother?..."
II Samuel 20:9

If you took a survey and asked all the people in your town whether or not they had perfect health, probably not many of them would answer "yes." We seldom meet a person who is really healthy. But, alas! how often we meet people with pale cheeks, dark circles under their eyes, overweight bodies, or a faltering step. Such manifestations say to us in unmistakable language, that that person does not have good health. He has a disease.

Go where we will throughout the world, we shall see that nearly the whole human family is in either a dying or a diseased condition. How it hurts the God of **love** to behold it all! He is *"touched with the feeling of our infirmities"* (Hebrews 4:15).

How sad to think that many people do not know how to regain their health or how to prevent what health they do have from being lost.

Exercise

What is Health? - Student - Page 1

Lack of Knowledge

"My people are destroyed for lack of knowledge...."
Hosea 4:6

There are five reasons why there is so much disease in the land. These reasons explain why so few human beings have perfect health and live a life free of disease even unto a ripe old age.

(1) The people do not understand what health is.

(2) They do not understand the conditions necessary to health.

(3) They do not understand the nature of disease.

(4) They do not understand the cause of disease.

(5) They are unwilling to forego a present pleasure for the sake of a future good.

Until people understand the first four reasons and have become willing to practice the last, we cannot expect to see much improvement in health matters. The object of this series on health is to learn about these things. Then we will be able to maintain our own health as well as reach out in **love** and help others understand how to regain theirs.

Our first question, then, should be, what is health?

What is Health? - Student - Page 2

Health Is...

"And God saw every thing that he had made, and behold, <u>it was very good</u>...."
Genesis 1:31

Simply said, health is the absence of disease. It is a condition of the body in which a person has no pain, but instead, has an undisturbed sense of well-being. Our **loving** Creator wants His children to feel wonderful every day! His heart's desire is for us to have a sound mind in a sound body.

Health means action, vital action. Health is the sum of all the actions of all the tissues, structures, and organs of the body when they perform their functions normally.

In the beginning, man was created with a perfectly balanced mind and all the organs of his body were perfectly developed. The mind and body were designed in such a way that they are dependent on each other for the full and proper use of each organ or faculty. *"For the body is not one member, but many....And whether one member suffer, all the members suffer with it; or one member be honored, all the members rejoice with it"* (I Corinthians 12:14, 26). Health is the condition of the body in which each organ performs its whole duty. In this state, there is an exact balance in the actions of the various tissues and structures of the person. The mind is also balanced and at peace through the influence of God's Spirit.

Adam and Eve were created with perfect minds and bodies.

Law of Love

"Charity [love]... Doth not behave itself unseemly...."
I Corinthians 13:4-5

If we want to learn about health we must study each of the parts of the body and the ministries they perform. God's law of self-sacrificing **love** is written on every nerve and fiber of our bodies. Each organ takes only to give. There is nothing, except the selfish heart of man, that lives to serve itself.

Health is Wealth

A clear, bright eye
That can pierce the sky
With the strength of an eagle's vision,
And a steady brain
That can bear the strain
And shock of the world's collision;

A well-knit frame,
With a ruddy flame
Aglow, and the pulses leaping
With the measured time
Of an inward rhyme,
Their beautiful record keeping;

A rounded cheek,
Where the roses speak
Of a soil that is rich for thriving,
And a chest so grand
That the lungs expand
Exultant, without the striving;

A breath like morn,
When the crimson dawn
Is fresh in its dewy sweetness;
A manner bright,
And a spirit light,
With joy at its full completeness,

O, give me these,
Nature's harmonies,
And keep all your golden treasures;
For what is wealth
To the boon of health
And its sweet attendant pleasures?
—Unknown

Health Questionnaire

1. How would you rate your health on this scale?

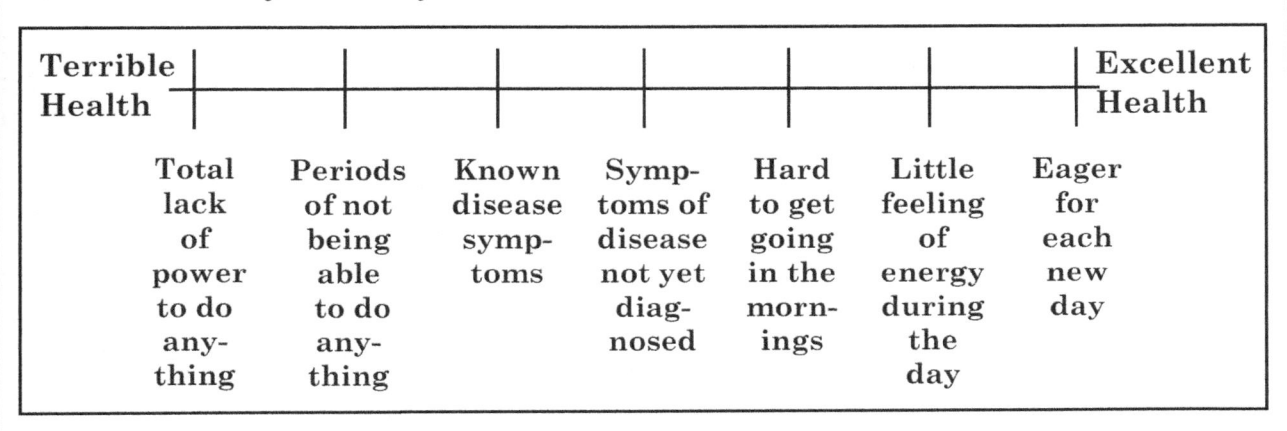

Terrible Health							Excellent Health
	Total lack of power to do anything	Periods of not being able to do anything	Known disease symptoms	Symptoms of disease not yet diagnosed	Hard to get going in the mornings	Little feeling of energy during the day	Eager for each new day

2. Do you know anyone who has (1) a robust frame with firm muscles and without extra fat, (2) erect posture, (3) clear mind, (4) cheerful spirits, (5) who can say with the keenest sense of enjoyment, "I am always well. Aches and pains and sickness to me are unknown?"

3. Do you overeat?

4. Do you enjoy physical activity to the point of perspiring every day?

5. Do you ever feel chilly or have cold skin on any body part?

6. Do you have a set mealtimes, bedtime, and arising time?

7. Do you have colds or stomach upsets?

8. Do you use caffeine (cola drinks, chocolate, and coffee)?

9. Do you fall asleep when sitting still?

11. Do you have pain or discomfort in head, trunk or extremities?

12. Do you have one or more bowel movements daily?

What is Health? - Student - Page 5

13. Do you have pale urine?

14. Do you have allergies, hayfever, or skin problems?

15. Do you have frequent infections or accidents?

16. Do you ever feel depressed or gloomy?

17. Are you maintaining your mental and spiritual health by daily Bible study and prayer?

Notes

The Importance of Good Health
"...All that a man hath will he give for his life."
Job 2:4

The first and greatest blessing that God bestows upon a person is life. This is the basis of all other blessings. Without it no other blessing could be enjoyed. Hence, the loss of life is the greatest punishment that can be inflicted upon a man. *"All that a man hath will he give for his life."* When life is at stake, everything sinks into insignificance in comparison.

Next to life, the greatest physical blessing a man can enjoy is good health. Without health, even life itself becomes useless, and sometimes even worse than useless—it becomes a burden and a curse. There are those all through the land who could agree to this. A man may have talents, wealth, friends, and everything that is desirable to make him happy and useful; yet if he is deprived of health, all these are of no value to him. He would give them all for sound health.

It is God's wish that we be happy, and we have no right to bring a moment's unhappiness on ourselves by transgression against or by neglect of His laws that preserve our health. We have work to do for one another, for the family and the neighborhood. We are not free to disqualify ourselves, or in any degree to cut short our power of usefulness, by interfering with our own health. The loss of health often makes one person a source of expense and trouble and grief to many. Each person will have to answer at the judgment bar of God for the far-reaching results of the neglect of his health.

Go to that invalid who has been in a wheelchair or lain upon a bed for years, and ask him the value of good health. Its price cannot be told. Money cannot buy it. Houses and lands cannot purchase it. Our simple salutations* show how important we regard it. When we meet a friend, the first sentence is, "How are you?" We regard this as the most important question we can ask. Everything depends upon it. God, in His holy word, has attached the same importance to good health that we do.

*greetings

What is Health? - Student - Page 7

Health and Talents

"The God Of Israel is he that giveth strength and power unto his people. Blessed be God."
Psalm 68:35

A "pound" of the energy that comes with good health with only an "ounce" of talent will achieve greater results than a "pound" of talent with an "ounce" of energy. In the same sense, a carpenter may have good tools, but what are these without strength of arm and hand? Even the mental talents (qualities of mind such as judgment, imagination, and eloquence) united with a healthy body can attain a force and splendor that would be impossible without good health.

The Birthright Blessing

"Because the carnal mind is enmity against God: for it is not subject to the law of God, neither indeed can be."
Romans 8:7

A healthy young child is a good illustration of how perfect health means positive enjoyment in living. Imagine a little fellow, as his **loving** mother lets him go outside to play fresh from his bath, his round cheeks polished like apples. Every step is a spring or a dance. He runs, he laughs, he shouts; his face breaks into a thousand dimpling smiles at a word. His breakfast of oatmeal and fruit is swallowed with an eager and incredible delight. In fact, it seems so good that he stops to laugh or thump the table now and then in expression of his joy. All day long he runs and frisks and plays. And when at night the little head seeks

What is Health? - Student - Page 8

the pillow, down go the eye-curtains of the body temple, and sleep comes without bad dreams. In the morning his first note is a crow or a laugh, as he sits up in his bed. He is the embodiment of joy, sunshine, music, and laughter for all the house.

How **loving** and generous the Author of life is to give so much energy and health to a child at the outset of life. How sad it is to look forward thirty years, when the same child, now a grown man, wakes in the morning with a dull, heavy head. Such may be the consequence of a bad diet or smoking, not to mention staying up late watching television. When it is time for a good breakfast to fuel the body for the day, he has no appetite but downs a cup of coffee instead which whips his poor abused body into action. Then with weary steps and a half-asleep brain he drives to work where he spends the day in a stuffy office. The birthright blessing of life and health has been thrown away little by little.

God meant for us to travel the whole journey of life free from sickness.

God meant for us to travel the whole journey of life free from sickness, with wonderful strength of body and mind to fulfill the duties of life. But He foresaw the emergency that sin would create. Therefore, our **loving** God has implanted in man's body living or recuperative* forces, whereby in most cases, he can regain his health after he has injured it by a violation of the laws of his being, if he will but return to, and continue in the obedience of these laws. But, since this requires some self-denial on one's part, only a few have the moral courage and strength to do it for *"the carnal mind is...not subject to the law of God, neither indeed can be."*

What is Health? - Student - Page 9

Ten Commandments of Health

1. Do not make a god of the stomach. (Philippians 3:19)

2. Do not bow down to appetite. (Romans 16:18), nor serve every impulse, feeling, or passion; for if you do, your transgression will be visited upon you in pain, sickness, disease, and death, (Galatians 6:7-8), and others will be caused to suffer also.

3. Do not use the strength of your mind and body in vain. (Isaiah 49:4) Remember that both are gifts, and if you squander them, you will not be guiltless.

4. Remember to rest after work. Remember that at least eight hours out of the twenty-four should be spent in restful sleep. Remember that the stomach needs at least five or six hours of rest from the end of one meal to the beginning of the next. Remember that when you do not give the stomach rest, you make all its servants; namely, the intestines, liver, pancreas, kidneys, and skin work harder; the brain cannot rest, and the heart has to work harder to pump the blood. Remember to enter into the rest of the Sabbath day (Exodus 20:8). Communion with God is vital to good health.

What is Health? - Student - Page 10

5. Honor, respect, and make a right use of all the things of nature that give you health, life, and surround you with happiness. Honor your body as being the dwelling-place of God. Respect every law of health. Make health your study, and a part of your religion. Obey all the laws of your nature, *"that thy days may be long upon the land which the Lord thy God giveth thee"* (Exodus 20:12).

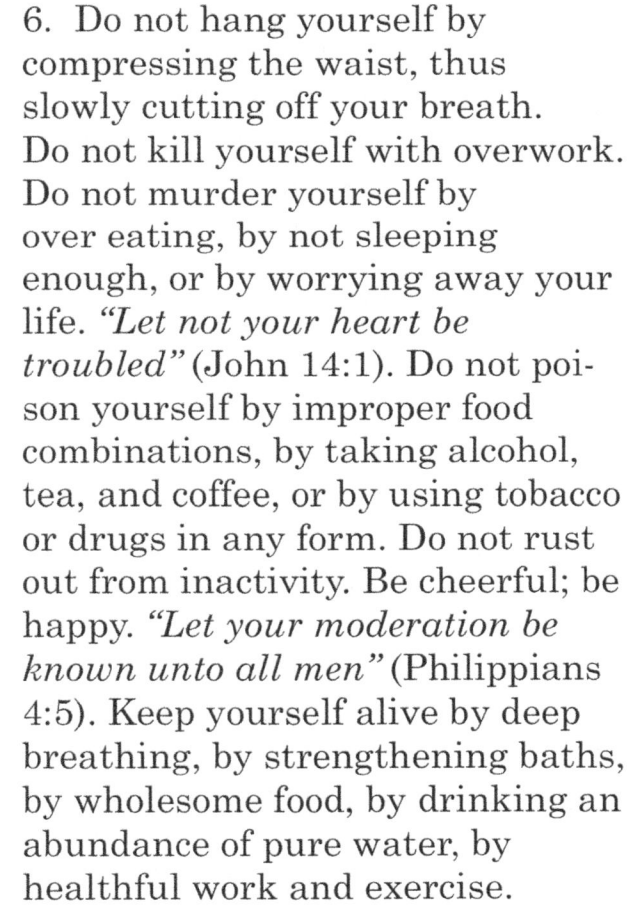

6. Do not hang yourself by compressing the waist, thus slowly cutting off your breath. Do not kill yourself with overwork. Do not murder yourself by over eating, by not sleeping enough, or by worrying away your life. *"Let not your heart be troubled"* (John 14:1). Do not poison yourself by improper food combinations, by taking alcohol, tea, and coffee, or by using tobacco or drugs in any form. Do not rust out from inactivity. Be cheerful; be happy. *"Let your moderation be known unto all men"* (Philippians 4:5). Keep yourself alive by deep breathing, by strengthening baths, by wholesome food, by drinking an abundance of pure water, by healthful work and exercise.

What is Health? - Student - Page 11

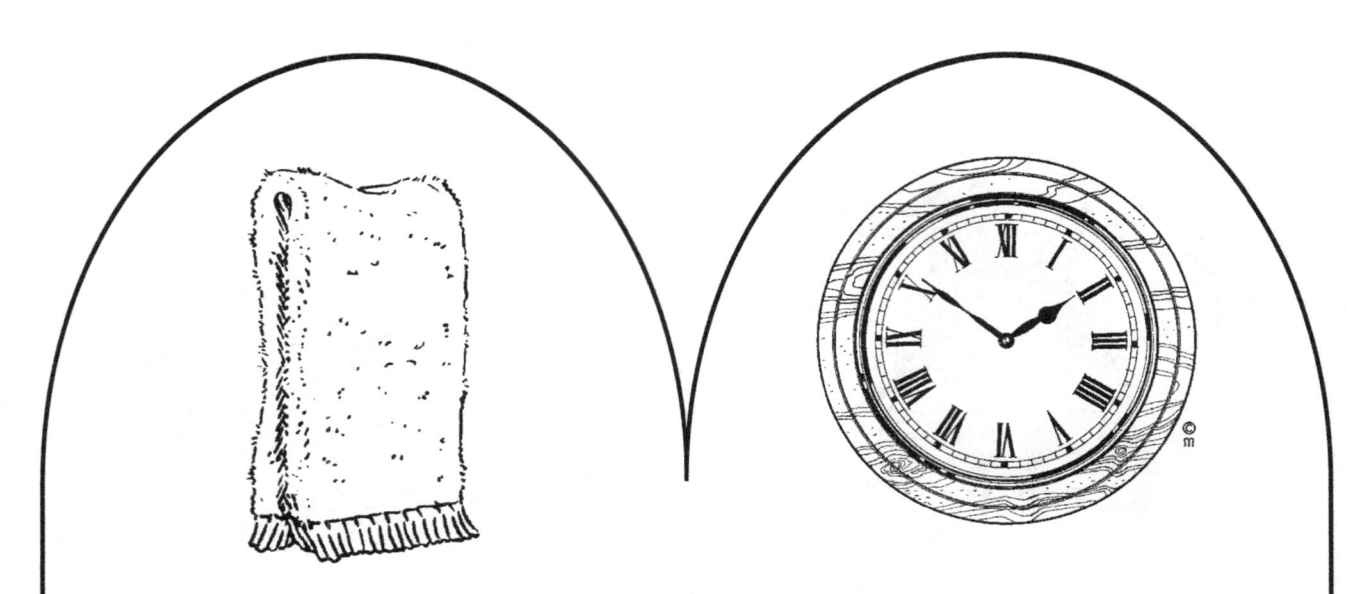

7. Be pure in your person (I Timothy 5:22). Let cleanliness be the first law of your life. Bathe daily, guard against all filth, avoid all stimulants and condiments, think noble thoughts, see the beautiful in all about you, and regard your body as sacred and not to be defiled.

8. Do not steal time from God by getting sick because of wrong habits of life on your part. Remember also that when you are sick, it takes the time of others to care for you. God wants all to be well so all may devote all their time and strength to His praise. Do not rob God of the life that He has entrusted to you for a wise purpose.

9. Do not deceive yourself by thinking you can sow "wild oats" for a time, or that you can violate natural law without a penalty. Nature cannot be deceived, though you may succeed in deceiving your friends.

10. Do not covet wealth or riches (even rich food) so that health is sacrificed to obtain it; for if you do, you will be more than willing to give all your wealth to regain the lost health. Do not harbor even a wish to do anything that others do which will act as a health-destroyer to you.

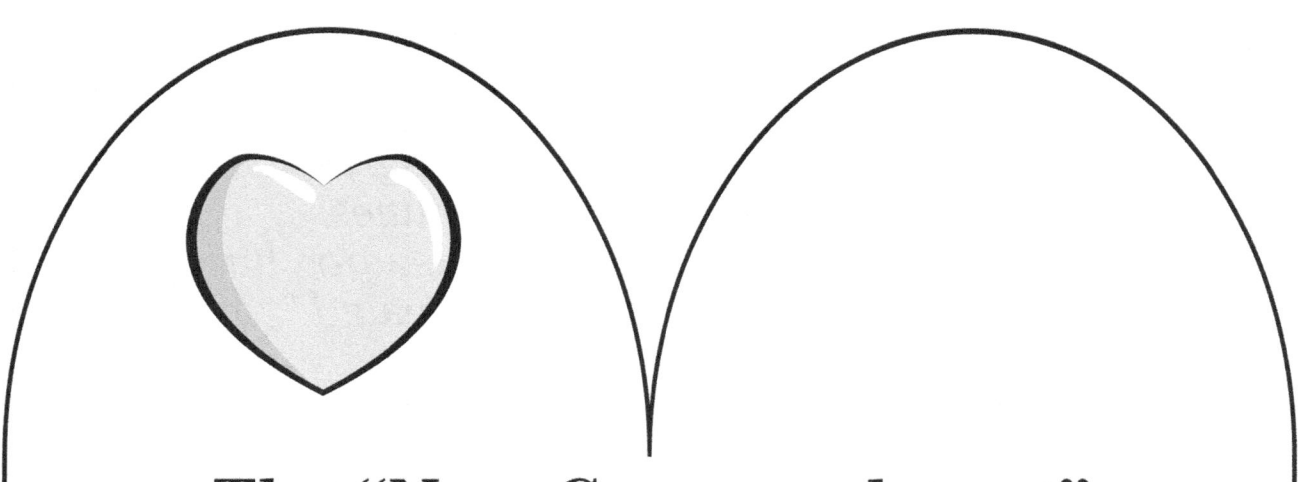

The "New Commandment"

Love the body of your neighbor as you **love** your own body. You **love** to enjoy health, you **love** to be well-fed, to be warm and clothed, to have shelter. It is right that all should **love** these blessings; but remember that if you **love** your neighbor as yourself, you will **love** to have him enjoy all these good things also, and will be willing to share them with him. Your **love** for yourself leads you to obtain these comforts; you should do likewise for your neighbor. *"Thou shalt love thy neighbor as thyself"* (Matthew 22:39).

—Adapted from
F.M. Rossiter, M.D.

Guard It

*"But he was wounded for our transgressions,
he was bruised for our iniquities:
the chastisement of our peace was upon him;
and with his stripes we are healed."*
Isaiah 53:5

Our health should be as sacredly guarded as our characters. It is easy for a person to lose his health, but it is much harder to regain it once lost. Christ purchased the right to restore our health by an infinite price. *"With his stripes we are healed."*

We can show our **love** for God by keeping ourselves in health. Then our minds will be clear to hear God's still, small voice, and our bodies will be energized to perform perfect, efficient service.

Reflect
Our Greatest Wealth

*Lord, we praise Thee for our health.
Truly it's our greatest wealth.
All of our strength comes from Thee,
And our cure from Calvary.*
—*Unknown*

What is Health? - Student - Page 14

Review

Place I - II - III

1. Draw the ten commandments of health below.

1.

2.

3.

4.

5.

6.

7.

8.

9.

10.

2. Unscramble the missing words.

Health is that condition of _____ and _____ which enables both to
                               YODB   DIMN
perform their _____ properly and without _____.
             TUSEID   NIAP

3. Health is the _____ of all the actions of all the tissues, structures, and organs of the body when they perform their functions _____ .

4. What did God create man with in the beginning? What does this tell you about God's desire for man today?

What is Health? - Student - Page 15

5. Who do you owe it to to preserve your health? Circle the correct letters.

a. your family
b. your neighborhood
c. your church
d. your community
e. God
f. yourself

6. This life is given us for _____ but we cannot do this
   RALOB
without _____ and _____.
          FILE   HLATEH

7. Your teacher may dictate the spelling words. Give an oral meaning of these words.

Place II - III

8. When we neglect to care for our health it is a sin of omission. Omission is "the neglect or failure to do something which a person had power to do, or which duty required to be done." Put an O by sins of omission or their results.

___ A. Gerald failed to put on his coat when he went outside to play and got a cold as a result.

___ B. Amy ate a candy bar between meals. The sugar in it lowered her resistance to the "flu" that was going around in the neighborhood. Amy got the "flu" and then her little brother caught it from her.

___ C. Johnny stepped in a mud puddle and got his feet wet on the way back from getting the mail. He did not take time to put on dry socks and shoes because Uncle Tom had already started the car to go to town and Johnny had permission to go with him.

___ D. Jill's father took a job where he worked seven days a week all year. After three years of hard work he had to take 6 months off from the job due to a nervous breakdown.

___ E. Marcie spent her allowance every week for candy even though she had a lot of dental fillings already. When a collection was taken at church for some starving people in Africa, Marcie did not have any money to contribute.

Health is Wealth

What is Health? - Student - Page 16

____ F. Jimmy failed to cover his mouth when he was coughing at his teacher's desk. The teacher got his cold and spread it to her grandfather who was living in her home. Grandfather was 95 years old and his cold turned into pneumonia and he was very sick.

____ G. Lana took some potato salad to the church picnic. She forgot to add ice to the cooler it was in. It was a hot day and several people got food-poisoning because they did not know the potato salad had been out of refrigeration too long and had grown bacteria in it that would make them sick.

9. What are the five reasons there is so much disease in the land?

10. If someone asked you, "Why do I need to be concerned about my health? Why can not I live any way I want to?" what would you say?

11. Our health should be as sacredly guarded as our _____.

12. What text expresses God's desire concerning our health?

13. What did Christ warn people about when He healed their diseases?

14. Health can be preserved only by _____.

15. The health of the body affects the _____ of the _____.

16. Explain the relationship between health and happiness.

17. Look back at the last several times you got sick. Can you identify the causes in each case?

What is Health? - Student - Page 17

Research
Actions of the Organs

"Those members of the body...."
I Corinthians 12:23

The action of each organ aids in the development, growth, and maintenance of the health of the body. These actions can be divided into two classes: (1) nutritive actions, and (2) cleansing actions. The nutritive actions change food into the tissues of the body. The cleansing actions purify the body by gathering up the worn-out material and casting it out of the body. When the nutritive actions and the cleansing actions are perfectly balanced, then the body is in health. When things get out of balance, there is disease. The more unbalanced the actions, the more serious the disease. According to the condition, the body can either waste away from lack of proper nutrition, or it can become polluted from a lack of purification.

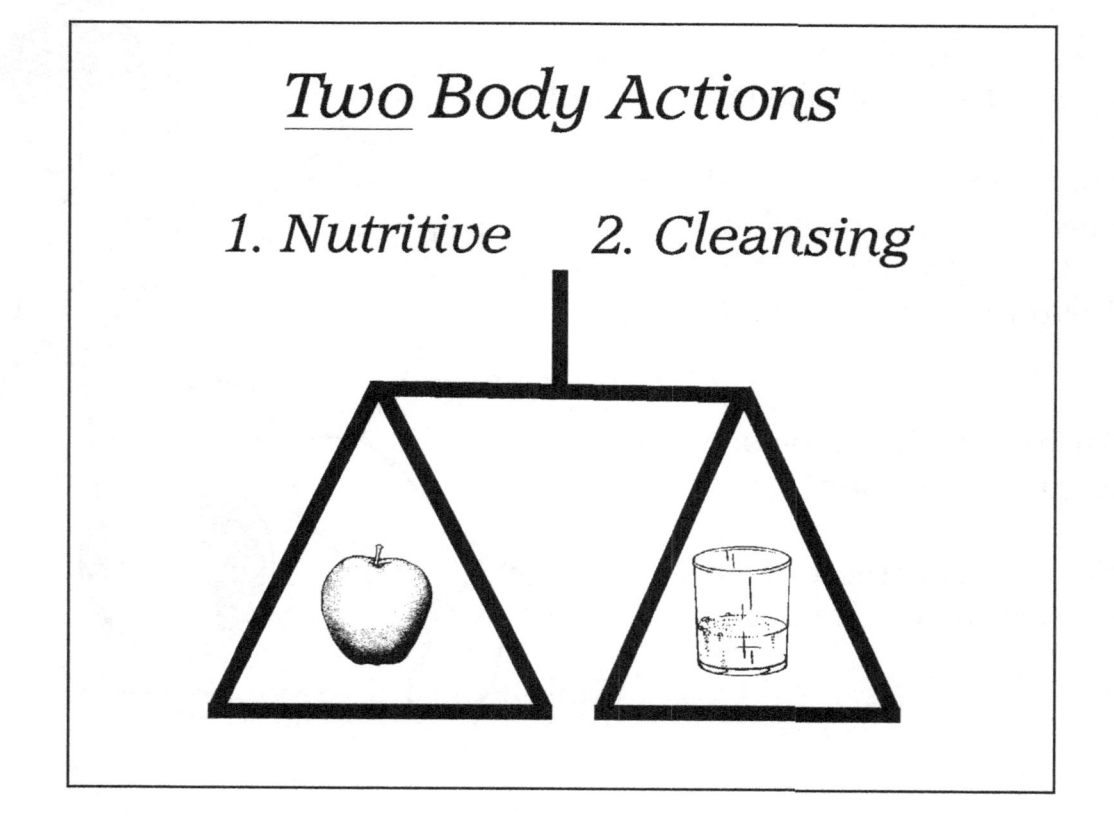

Two Body Actions

1. Nutritive   2. Cleansing

Remedying a Problem

"Behold, I will bring it health and cure, and I will cure them, and will reveal unto them the abundance of peace and truth."
Jeremiah 33:6

What do you think happens when a person breaks one of the laws of health and it results in one of the organs of the body not being able to do its proper share of the work? Well, in that case, some other organ takes on the extra work. This can remind us of our Bible lesson. Jesus lovingly came to perform the extra work of redemption that became necessary when the members of His body did not do what they should have done. "Now ye are the body of Christ, and members in particular" (I Corinthians 12:27). Christ responds lovingly when His body is out of harmony. He says: "Behold, I will bring it health and cure, and I will cure them, and will reveal unto them the abundance of peace and truth."

The extra work the organs must do to make up for the ones that are not functioning properly is a strain on them. Usually, all the energy of each organ is used for the purpose of keeping the body in a normal state. In a normal condition, there is a harmonious action of all the organs of the body and mind that results in a pleasant feeling of energy. The body can then successfully resist getting sick.

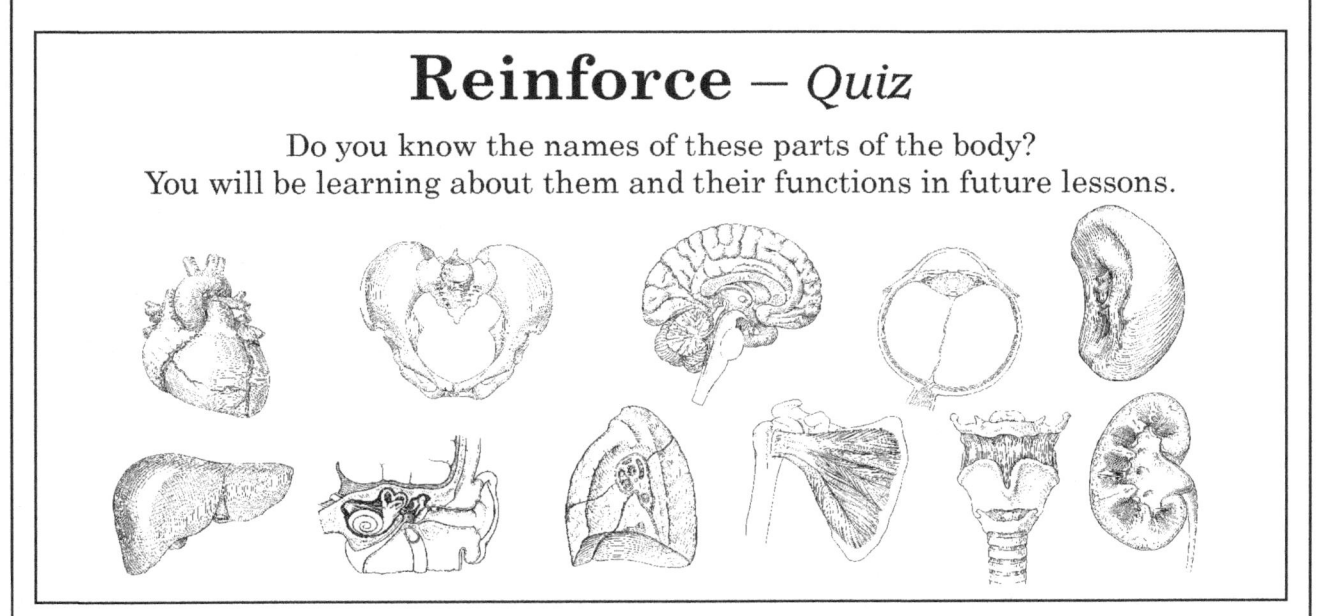

Reinforce – *Quiz*

Do you know the names of these parts of the body?
You will be learning about them and their functions in future lessons.

What is Health? - Student - Page 19

Review

Place I - II - III

1. What can cause the organs to fall behind in their work?

2. What happens if one of the organs is not able to do its proper share of the work?

3. What causes an organ to be strained?

Place II - III

4. In a normal state of health there is a _____ action of all the organs of the body and mind that results in a _____ _____ of _____.

5. When the body has plenty of _____ it is able to resist _____ _____.

6. What does this text imply about disease? "The diseased have ye not strengthened, neither have ye healed that which was sick" (Ezekiel 34:4).

7. What two body actions help keep us in health?

8. What condition results in disease?

Place III

9. How could eating too much good food cause disease?

_____
_____
_____
_____
_____
_____
_____
_____

What is Health? - Student - Page 20

Remind

1. When breathing in oxygen in the air, be reminded of the nutritive actions of the body in maintaining health. When breathing out waste gas, think of the cleansing actions the body makes.

2. Notice how people carry their bodies when they are thinking sad thoughts. Their bodies sympathize with their minds.

3. Be a sunbeam of love in your family, neighborhood, and church. This will help your health as well as others because a loving, smiling face is contagious. *"A merry heart doeth good like a medicine"* (Proverbs 17:22).

4. Playing on a see-saw at the park can bring to mind the balance that is necessary between the nutritive and cleansing actions in order for the body to be in perfect health.

5. When carrying table scraps to the compost pile, consider how each family member has a part to play in contributing to the health of the family as a whole just as each organ does for the body.

6. Sing the hymn, "Sunlight in the Heart."

6. Read the story, "Every Attention but One."

Reflect

"A merry heart doeth good like a medicine."

Sing This Song

Sunlight In The Heart

"I will be glad and rejoice in thee..." (Psalm 9:1).

Arr. by F. E. Belden

Melody by M.T. Haughey Arr.

1. There is sun-light on the hill-top, There is sun-light on the sea,
And the gold-en beams are sleep-ing, On the soft and ver-dant lea;
But a rich-er light is fill-ing All the cham-bers of my heart;

2. In the dust I leave my sad-ness, As the garb of oth-er days,
For Thou rob-est me with glad-ness, And Thou fill-est me with praise;
And to that bright home of glo-ry Which Thy love hath won for me,

3. Lov-ing Sav-iour, Thou hast bought me, And my life, my all, is Thine;
Let the lamp Thy love has light-ed To Thy praise and glo-ry shine;
And to that bright home of glo-ry Which Thy love hath won for me,

Sunlight In The Heart (2)

For Thou dwell-est there my Sav-iour, And 'tis sun-light where Thou art.
In my heart and mind as-cend-ing, My glad spir-it fol-lows Thee.
In my heart and mind as-cend-ing, My glad spir-it fol-lows Thee.

Refrain

O the sun-light! beau-ti-ful sun-light! O the sun-light in the heart!

Je-sus' smile can ban-ish sad-ness; It is sun-light in the heart.

Every Attention but One

Just as the organs help one another in disease so should family members aid each other when one member is sick.

The family sat in the library, a little anxious-eyed. The doctor stood in the doorway. "Your aunt is just worn out, that is all. She must have absolute quiet and rest for a while, and have appetizing meals served to her. She must be given tender, loving care. One of you girls should be made a sort of bodyguard and attendant for her, to amuse her, read to her, run errands for her, and look after her person and her room. She needs someone with her constantly. What she needs is perfect freedom from annoyance, irritation, and excitement. She will be better than ever at the end of a month like that."

Then the doctor went out, and the family talked it over. "It is a fortunate thing that I took the first-aid course, isn't it? I'll be able to give Aunt Emily the very best of attention now. I'll move a cot into that little alcove in her room, and take up my head-quarters there. It will be just what Aunt Emily needs, and it will be fine training for me. Mrs. Alcott said the best way to become proficient in serving the sick is by actual practice." So spoke Olive, the oldest daughter.

It must be confessed that the family was a little dubious about this plan. "Don't you think Violet could do it better?" suggested the father.

"Why, Father!" Olive's voice was very indignant. "Why should Violet do it? She hasn't had any training in nursing at all. And she is the youngest daughter—"

"Violet is so even-tempered and cheery," continued the father. "It seems to me she would be very comfortable in a sick room. Of course, she has not had the training—but cheer is a big thing for a sick person."

"I am the oldest; I have had training, and it seems to me I ought to be in charge."

In the end, Olive had her way. Aunt Emily herself was not asked.

The doctor often talked with Aunt Emily. He watched her closely. He also watched Olive as she went about her work. She did not neglect the duties that came to her, that was evident. The room was spotlessly clean, and always sunny. The bed linens were immaculate. Aunt Emily herself seemed to be receiving every attention. But the doctor was not satisfied. In spite of good food, much rest, entire quiet and relaxation, Aunt Emily did not improve. What was the matter?

He watched Olive's attitude toward her aunt, and observed every look and every movement. Finally he was convinced that he knew what was wrong. When he left that day, he motioned to Olive to follow him. "My dear," he said, kindly but very firmly, "I want you to let your sister take your place here for a few days—the little plump one—what is her name? Yes, Violet. I want you to turn everything over to Violet for a while. A change is sometimes good for a patient."

"Why, Doctor, have I been doing so badly?"

"No, you have worked hard, you have kept the room perfectly clean, you have read, you have served meals. But now let the other one try it."

Olive was hurt. "I am sure Aunt Emily has no reason to complain. I have given her every possible attention."

Olive was banished, and Violet was sent in to her aunt, to take her sister's place. And again the doctor watched. It must be confessed that the room was a little less orderly. For instance, the long muslin curtains were generally drawn back away from the window, and thrust over the corner of a picture. The doctor's eye rested upon them more than once. Aunt Emily explained promptly: "I like to feel the breeze coming in full and strong, and I do not like to see curtains blowing back and forth. And I do like to give the sunshine a broad sweep at me. It wrinkles the curtains badly, and looks untidy, but I wanted it, and of course Violet fixed them for me." The doctor smiled.

One afternoon he dropped in unexpectedly. The room and the patient were unpresentable, to say the least. A comb and brush lay on the white coverlet. The two were eating apples, and two unsightly cores were on the dresser tray. Aunt Emily only laughed at the doctor's expression. "Violet was just ready to brush my hair, when I happened to think of the apples. But never mind, Doctor, she'll brush it nicely when you're gone."

"Did you forget your medicine at two o'clock?"

"I forgot all about it," declared Aunt Emily, laughing again.

"I remembered it," said Violet, "but I remembered you said it was better for one to be interested and amused than to take countless bottles of medicine, so I just brought in the apples."

"Quite right," said the doctor. Then he added, "As I explained to you, medicine is the least essential part of your aunt's treatment. If anyone accuses you of neglecting your patient, Miss Violet, send him to me."

"A cheerful heart doeth good like a medicine," said Aunt Emily, softly, turning fond eyes upon her loving young niece.

"Exactly," answered the doctor.

"As I explained to you, medicine is the least essential part of your aunt's treatment."

What is Health? - Student - Page 26

Reflect
Causes

"...The curse causeless shall not come."
Proverbs 26:2

Our sufferings and miseries, our aches and pains mostly arise from one of these things:

   A. False ideas
   B. Wrong habits
   C. Perverted* tastes
   D. Mistakes in relating ourselves to our conditions

Using the letters above, see if you can identify the cause of the following health problems.

___ 1. Mr. Jones got lung cancer after smoking for 20 years.

___ 2. When Jamie was visiting his uncle, he took him to the cafeteria for lunch. Jamie chose a sugary dessert instead of fresh strawberries.

___ 3. Harold wanted to go when the neighborhood children were leaving to go fly kites in the park one windy and chilly March day. In order to catch up with them Harold rushed out without his windbreaker on. As a result of getting chilled that day, he came with a cold.

___ 4. Mr. Lacey drinks a cup of coffee before work in the morning to perk himself up. He says it gives him energy.

___ 5. Jenny eats only healthful foods but she likes to snack between meals on fruit. The body cannot make pure blood out of foods that are imperfectly digested (which is what happens when food is eaten between meals).

Which is more healthful?

This   or   this?

*turned from a proper use to a wrong use

What is Health? - Student - Page 27

Drugs and Disease

"...In vain shalt thou use many medicines; for thou shalt not be cured."
Jeremiah 46:11

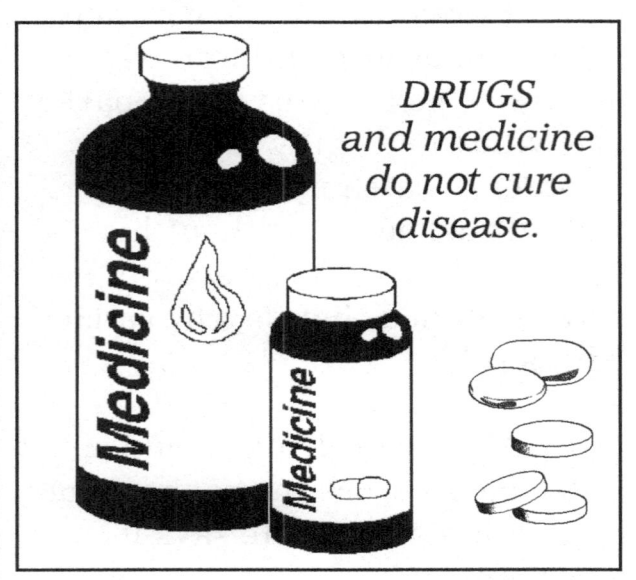

DRUGS and medicine do not cure disease.

Drugs and medicine do not cure disease. It is true that they sometimes offer relief for a while, and the patient appears to recover as the result of their use. But the reason for this is that nature has enough vital force to get rid of the drug and to correct the bad conditions that caused the disease. Health is recovered in spite of the drug. But in most cases the drug only changes the form and location of the disease. Often the effect of the drug seems to be overcome for a time, but the results remain in the system and can work harm later on.

Nature's Effort

"Is there no balm in Gilead; is there no physician there? why then is not the health of the daughter of my people recovered?"
Jeremiah 8:22

Every dose of drugs lowers the vitality of the patient. Always remember that God's restorative power is in nature, not in drugs. **Disease is actually an effort of nature to free the system from conditions that result from a violation of the laws of health.** Disease may be considered a process of purification and repair. In case of sickness, the cause should be looked for. Unhealthful conditions should be changed, wrong habits corrected. Then nature is to be assisted in her effort to expel impurities and to re-establish right conditions in the system. Natural remedies help nature out. They work along with her efforts to set things back in order in the body temple.

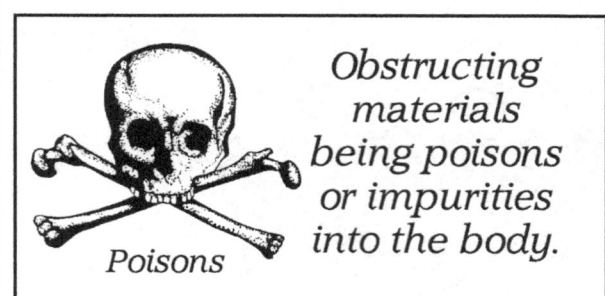

Poisons — Obstructing materials being poisons or impurities into the body.

What is Health? - Student - Page 28

Natural Remedies

*"A merry heart doeth good like a medicine:
but a broken spirit drieth the bones."*
Proverbs 17:22

Diseases are often caused by obstructions,* the obstructing materials being poisons or impurities of some kind. Natural remedies help remove the obstructions and leave the body healthy. Pure air, sunlight, temperance, rest, exercise, proper diet, the use of water, trust in divine power—these are the true remedies. Every person should have a knowledge of nature's remedial agencies and how to apply them. Natural remedies are materials and influences which have normal relations to the body organs. Drugs have abnormal relations to the body. These the body must resist and expel if possible. The true healing art consists in supplying the living system with any of the natural remedies it can use under the circumstance, and not in using poisons it must resist and try to get rid of.

The use of natural remedies requires an amount of care and effort that many are not willing to give. Nature's process of healing and upbuilding is gradual, and to the impatient it seems slow. The surrender of hurtful indulgences requires sacrifice. But in the end it will be found that nature, untrammeled, does her work wisely and well. Those who persevere in obedience to her laws will reap the reward in health of body and health of mind.

8 Naturals

Pure Air   Exercise
Sunlight   Proper Diet
Temperance   Water
Rest   Trust

*something that gets in the way

Temperance

*A synonym for temperance is abstemiousness.
It has to do with eating sparingly and refraining from alcoholic beverages and other harmful substances.*

Water is the best drink!

What is Health? - Student - Page 29

Review
Place I - II - III

1. List the eight natural remedies below.
   Draw an illustration of each in the space provided.

Eight Natural Remedies
The True Remedies

1. _____   5. _____

2. _____   6. _____

3. _____   7. _____

4. _____   8. _____

2. Memorize the poem on the next page.

What is Health? - Student - Page 30

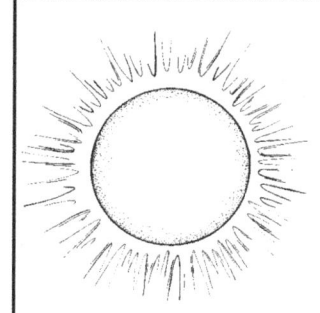

Our Eight Natural Doctors

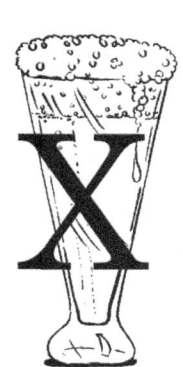

The best eight doctors you'll find anywhere,
Their services are an absolute must,
Are sunlight, water, proper diet, air,
Exercise, rest, temperance, and trust.

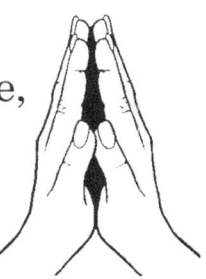

These eight doctors will surely bring you aid;
They work together with the laws God made.
Your sickness and ills they soon will mend,
And a fortune you will not have to spend.

—*Unknown*

Memorize this poem.

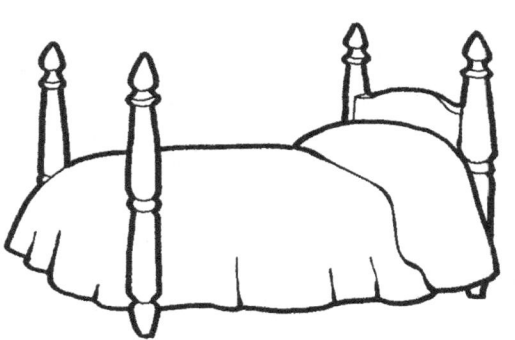

Rule of Thumb:

Do not use any remedy for disease that could make a well person sick.

What is Health? - Student - Page 31

Do You Know the Secret to Good Health?

*"For as he thinketh in his heart, so is he:
Eat and drink, saith he to thee; but his heart is not with thee."*
Proverbs 23:7

The Bible has the answer in Leviticus 17:11. It says *"The life of the flesh is in the blood."* If we desire good health we must have good, pure blood. All the laws of health are important because they either help the body make good blood, or help purify the blood, or help make sure the blood gets to all parts of the body unhindered. It would not do much good if you had pure blood that did not circulate freely and nourish all parts of your body. So the main goal as far as aiming at perfect health is to have pure blood and perfect circulation.

Let us look briefly at each of the eight natural remedies and see how they relate to the secret of good health.

Pure air – provides oxygen, a "food" for the cells, through the bloodstream.

Sunlight – purifies the bloodstream.

Temperance – keeps harmful substances out of the blood stream; keeps it from becoming clogged with toxic by products of overeating.

Exercise – cleanses the bloodstream.

Proper Diet – makes healthy blood that will build up the health of the entire body.

Use of Water – cleanses the tissues through the blood stream.

Rest – helps rebuilds the cells of the body.

Trust in Divine Power – brings about positive emotions that affect the hormones that circulate in the bloodstream.

"Sickness of the mind prevails everywhere. <u>Nine tenths</u> of the diseases from which men suffer have their foundation here."*

In the Garden of Eden God **lovingly** provided man with all the benefits contained in the eight natural remedies. The same remedies that repair the body and get

*Mind, Character, and Personality 59

it well are also the things that keep a healthy body sound.

Assignment – Read the creation story in Genesis and see if you can identify the elements of the eight natural remedies.

"And the Lord God formed man of the dust of the ground, and breathed into his nostrils the breath of life; and man became a living soul" (Genesis 2:7). Man was made out of the dust of the ground and God gave him the proper diet that would match the chemical elements from which he was made.

What was the diet God gave man? Read Genesis 1:29 and Genesis 2:16. Then find a sample of this diet in your kitchen.

    Country living is the best way to secure all the elements of good health. That is why God placed Adam and Eve in a garden setting. Do we **love** and trust God enough today to follow the principles of a healthy lifestyle as illustrated in the garden of Eden? *"According to your faith be it unto you"* (Matthew 9:29). *"Whatsoever a man soweth, that shall he also reap"* (Galatians 6:7).

Review
Place II-III

1. If we want to have good health or overcome illness, we must have _____ _____ and _____ _____.

Disease comes from _____ _____ and imperfect _____.

2. What spiritual parallel can you make about the blood being the key to life and health? _____
_____
_____
_____

Place I
color this picture.

What is Health? - Student - Page 33

Match

3. Match the remedy with one of its effects.

1. temperance

A. provides oxygen which helps burn up impurities in the body

2. rest

B. purifying rays kill germs and charge the body with energy

3. sunlight

C. keeps the body strong

4. pure air

D. provides good building materials for growth and repair

5. proper diet

E. cleanses the tissues, inside and out

6. use of water

F. frees the mind from the health-destroying emotions of guilt and fear

7. trust in divine power

G. if the body's energy is not wasted on harmful indulgences there is enough energy left over to heal and repair the body

8. exercise

H. this gives the body undisturbed time to build up its strength

What is Health? - Student - Page 34

The Praise of Good Doctors

The best of all the pill-box crew,
    Since ever time began,
Are the doctors who have the most to do
    With the health of a hearty man.

And so I count them up again
    And praise them as I can;
      There's Dr. Diet,
      And Dr. Quiet,
      And Dr. Merryman.

There's Dr. Diet, he tries my tongue.
    "I know you well," says he:
"Your stomach is poor, and your liver is sprung.
    We must make your food agree."

And Dr. Quiet, he feels my wrist,
    And he gravely shakes his head:
"Now, now, dear sir, I must insist
    That you go at eight to bed."

But Dr. Merryman for me,
    Of all the pill-box crew!
For he smiles and says, as he takes the fee:
    "Laugh on, whatever you do!"

So now I eat what I ought to eat,
    And at eight I go to bed,
And I laugh in the face of cold or heat;
    For thus have the doctors said!

And so I count them up again,
    And praise them as I can:
      There's Dr. Diet,
      And Dr. Quiet,
      And Dr. Merryman.
        —*Unknown*

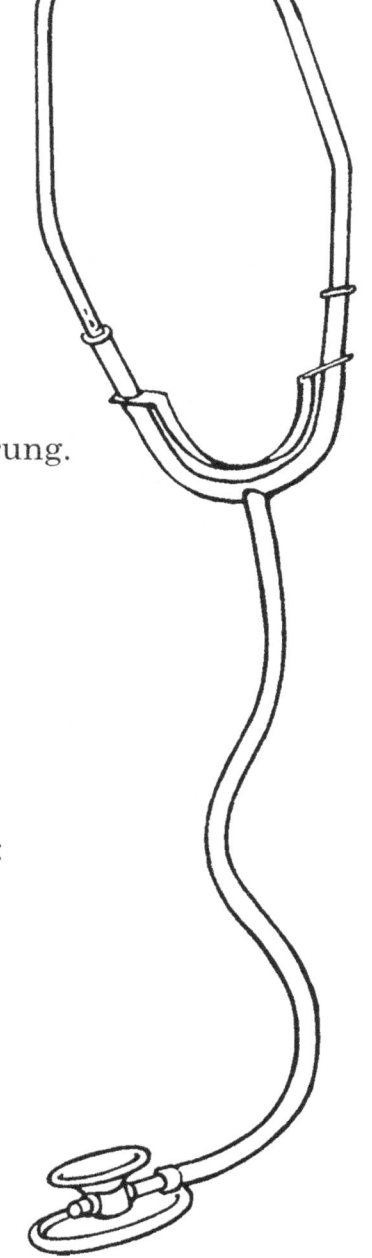

Research
Sickness and Disease

"Is any sick among you?..."
James 5:14

A person may not feel any pain or sickness and yet be diseased. It is sad to say, but many people become so diseased as to be beyond recovery (short of a miracle) before they even realize that there is something seriously wrong with them. For instance, perhaps you have heard of someone who was shocked to find out that cancer had made fearful inroads into his or her body.

Sickness is different than disease in that we generally only call a person sick when they have marked symptoms that something is wrong with their body. But a person may have a diseased action in some organ and yet that action may differ so slightly from the healthy action so as not to be noticed by them, much less by others. This is why it is so important for us to learn about the organs of our bodies. We will be doing this in the lessons that follow.

Copy the definition for these words. Use a dictionary.

Sickness -
_____
_____
_____
_____

Disease -
_____
_____
_____
_____

Sickness is a danger signal that nature hangs out when we have left her path, and are standing on forbidden ground.

What is Health? - Student - Page 36

Review
Place I

1. Transgression, or breaking the laws of health, brings affliction.*
Copy Psalm 107:17 below.

*affected with continued or often repeated pain, either of body or mind.

What is Health? - Student - Page 37

Review
Place II-III

2. Choose the best answers.

Disease is:

a. something you take a pill to get rid of

b. the effort of the body to free itself from unhealthful conditions

c. an unnatural condition of the body

3. Match the diseased or abnormal condition with how the body is trying to free itself from conditions that result from a violation of the laws of health.

- Cough

- Fever

- Sneeze

- Painful redness and swelling (inflammation)

- Chills

- Pimples

a. body's efforts to burn up impurities

b. body's effort to get rid of impurities through the skin

c. body's effort to free itself from too much mucous

d. body's efforts to bring more blood and nutrition to an injured area

e. body's efforts to warm itself

f. body's effort to cleanse the passages of the nose

4. What is the difference between sickness and disease?

Remind

1. When Mother or Father is burdened with too much to do, offer a helping hand. Think of how the members of the body assist one another when necessary.

2. Learn more about natural remedies that assist the body in freeing the system from conditions that result from a violation of the laws of health.

3. Visit the sick or send **loving** get-well cards to them.

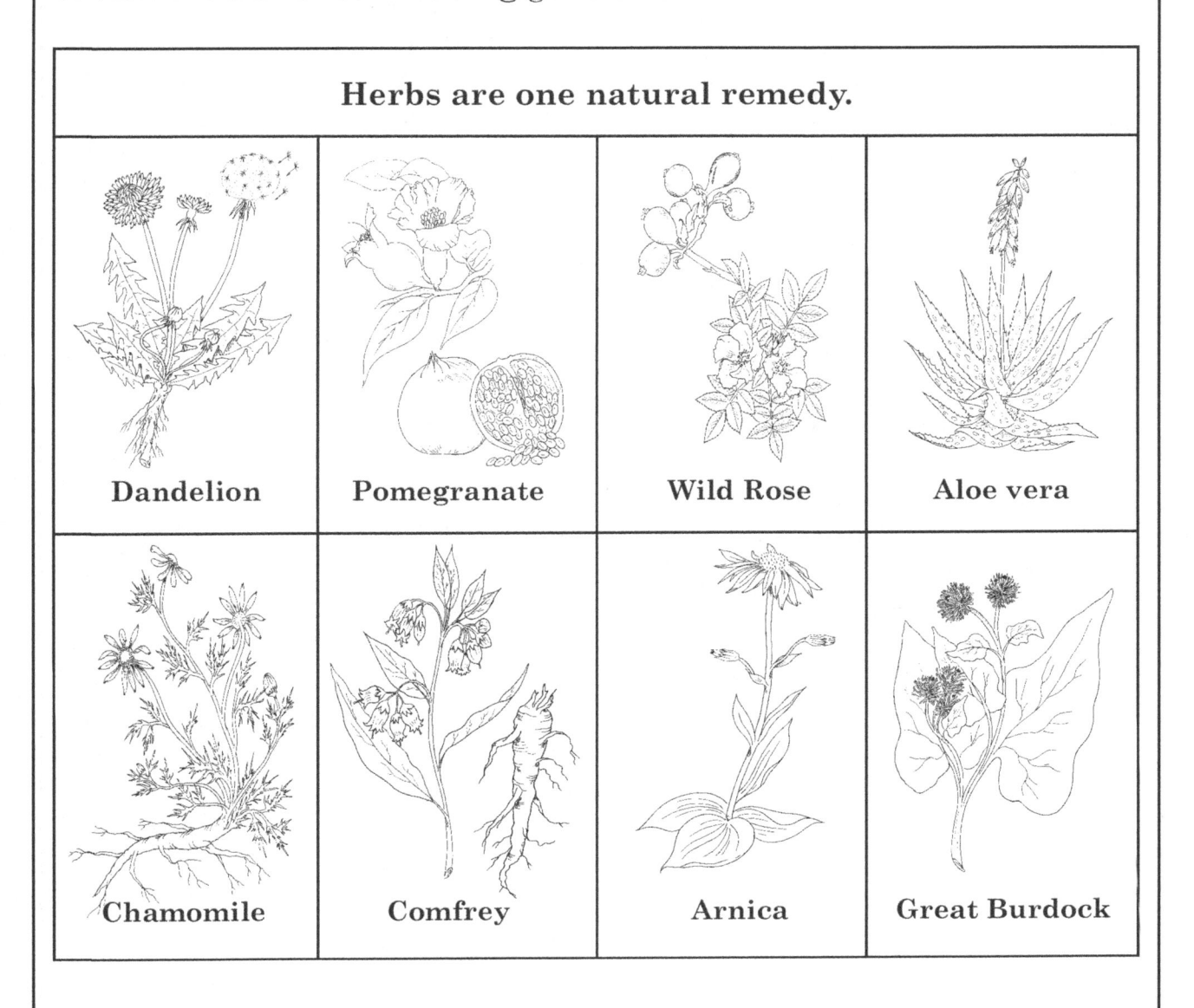

Herbs are one natural remedy.			
Dandelion	Pomegranate	Wild Rose	Aloe vera
Chamomile	Comfrey	Arnica	Great Burdock

What is Health? - Student - Page 39

Research – Vital Capital*

"And Moses was a hundred and twenty years old when he died: his eye was not dim, nor his natural force abated."
Deuteronomy 34:7

The question is often asked by someone who is trying to regain his health, "Why do not I get well faster?" He forgets that he has been years and years in breaking down. He has been drawing upon his vital capital until he is nearly bankrupt. What is the vital capital of the body and what part does it play in our health? Vital capital is what the Bible calls *"natural force."* (Deuteronomy 34:7) Every organ of the body has a certain amount of force or energy kept in store for future or special use. It uses this accumulated energy to meet the various emergencies which are sure to arise in life.

Write the concordance definitions for the bold words in Deuteronomy 34:7. *"His eye was not dim, nor his natural **force abated**."*

force _____

_____

abated _____

_____

*accumulated wealth, especially as used to produce more wealth

> *Your body organs are like energy savings' banks.*

To understand the natural force of the organs, consider the following example. The normal heartbeat of an adult is considered to be seventy times per minute. But in the case of an emergency, it is able to beat about one hundred and forty-five times per minute. Without this reserve** capacity, very slight causes of excitement or taxing labor would disturb the heart so much that a person would die from a heart attack. So it is with the stomach, liver, lungs, and various other organs of the body—each is made capable of doing an amount of work much greater than the ordinary requirements. A rich holiday dinner may give the digestive organs a lot of extra work, but if it comes only once a year, the extra strain may be endured without serious injury. But suppose a person has rich dinners every day. Because the reserve force equals the demand placed upon the organs, they may not see any bad effects for awhile.

**to be kept in store for future or special use

What is Health? - Student - Page 40

Since the body is not complaining about the extra load, the person may think it is all right to continue eating richly. *"Because sentence against an evil work is not executed speedily, therefore the heart of the sons of men is fully set in them to do evil"* (Ecclesiastes 8:11). By and by though, when the person has eaten no larger or richer dinner than usual, it is followed by an attack of indigestion from which they do not recover. The person may have had such attacks before, and has always gotten over them in a few days, and he does not understand why such is not the case now. The fact is, he has overdrawn his stock of vital capital, and he must take the consequences.

Nature allows us quite a bit of leeway. We do not have to walk in a line as narrow or straight as the top of a board fence, but the narrower and straighter we walk, the further we can go and the better it will be for us.

To illustrate more clearly what is meant by vital capital, imagine that a young man had a very large fortune left to him by his rich father, the amount of which he does not know. It is on deposit in a bank. He writes checks upon it whenever he wants to, and they are all honored, whether for $1,000.00 or for $10.00. He gambles with the capital and also indulges in expensive sinful practices that waste his body's energy. Some years pass. He writes a check one day for a thousand dollars, and it is cashed as usual. The next day he tries to draw out $100.00 and his check is not honored. He is angry and rushes down and demands a reason from the cashier why this small check is not cashed when he made one the day before for $1,000.00 which was honored. After all, he reasons, he had frequently written checks for $10,000.00 without any problems. The cashier explains to him that his capital has all been drawn out except for $50.00. He can have that amount if he desires, but no more.

"In thine hand is power and might; and in thine hand it is... to give strength unto all."
I Chronicles 29:12

What is Health? - Student - Page 41

In the same manner, the withdrawal made by bad habits upon nature's reserve force often is not felt in early life, but tells most seriously near its close. And this explains why a breakdown is often blamed on some little thing, losing sight of the real one. The man with the fortune could just as well say that it was his last check for $100.00 which reduced him to poverty, as the man who had eaten rich holiday dinners every day of his life could say that it was the last big meal he ate which caused all his following pain and discomfort. His vital capital is gone, and if he would build it up again, it must be by slow degrees, the same as the man who had only $50.00 left, would have to retrieve his fortune, if it could be done at all, by a series of slow and careful savings and investments.

"Because sentence against an evil work is not executed speedily, therefore the heart of the sons of men is fully set in them to do evil."
Ecclesiastes 8:11

Reflect

FACT

Most chronic* degenerative** diseases are caused by little transgressions often repeated.

*continuing for a long time **passing from a good to a worse state; losing former normal or higher qualities

What is Health? - Student - Page 42

Accounted For

I am not feeling well today,
    But why I cannot see.
I had some ice-cream yesterday
    And pancakes syrupy.

I also had some caramels
    And sugared almonds too.
And when I met with Tommy Wells
    Of his mints I had a few.

But I was careful with each one
    Too much of none I ate.
It cannot be that honey-bun,
    And yet the pain is great.

I had six cookies, but I've had
    Six cookies oft before:
They've never left me feeling bad
    Nor pickles—three or more.

    The soda-pop, it couldn't make
        Me ill—'twas Billie's treat
    I sort of think this fearful ache
        Comes wholly from the heat.
          —*Unknown*

Review
Place I

Color then read these words.

"It is good for me that I have been afflicted; that I might learn thy statutes.*"

Psalm 119:71

I II III IV   V VI VII VIII IX X

*appointed, bound (of quantity, labor or usage), commandment, law

What is Health? - Student - Page 44

Research
The Point of No Return

*"Turn ye from your evil ways;
for why will ye die?"*
Ezekiel 33:11

People often find their health failing, but think they have no time now to spend to improve it. Not a day passes that some do not pass a point, in the preying of disease upon their systems, beyond which there is no return. Yesterday they might have followed good advice and pursued a course which would have prolonged their lives for years; but today it is too late. Their bad habits have been so long pursued, and disease has reached so far, that there is not enough vitality left for healthy action to again take place (short of a miracle). The work of destruction will go on until the life-current ceases to flow. And a large portion of a life that might have been prolonged for many years, is cut short.

Many people start out with sufficient vitality to live in the enjoyment of good health for at least *"threescore years and ten"* (Psalm 90:10). But almost from birth the little one is treated in a manner that cuts off from its life some portion of its allotted time. Every child at its birth has power to reach a certain age, barring accidents, if all his habits through life are in accordance with the laws of health. But by certain unhealthful habits, even in very early childhood, the person's power to arrive at this age is shortened, and it is unalterably fixed that he can never regain what has been lost. And with most individuals these unhealthy habits are continued through life, so that instead of living to be healthy until their death at age 70, we see people getting diseases in middle age with sickness frequent in the younger years. This is no way to live or to die. For those who must die before Jesus returns there is something better than a disease—caused suffering which leads to death. Job 21:23 tells us about it. *"One dieth in his full strength, being wholly at ease and quiet."*

Turn ye, Turn ye, Turn ye, Turn ye, Turn ye, Turn ye, Turn ye.

Harken

"If thou wilt diligently hearken to the voice of the Lord thy God, and wilt do that which is right in his sight, and wilt give ear to his commandments, and keep all his statutes, I will put none of these diseases upon thee, which I have brought upon the Egyptians...."
Exodus 15:26

First 10 Generations

Adam – 930 years
"And all the days that Adam lived were nine hundred and thirty years: and he died" (Genesis 5:5).

Seth – 912 years
"And all the days of Seth were nine hundred and twelve years: and he died" (Genesis 5:8).

Enos – 905 years
"And all the days of Enos were nine hundred and five years: and he died" (Genesis 5:11).

Cainan – 910 years
"And all the days of Cainan were nine hundred and ten years: and he died" (Genesis 5:14).

Mahalaleel – 895 years
"And all the days of Mahalaleel were eight hundred ninety and five years: and he died" (Genesis 5:17).

Jared – 962 years
"And all the days of Jared were nine hundred sixty and two years: and he died" (Genesis 5:20).

Enoch – 365 years; translated, still alive
"And all the days of Enoch were three hundred sixty and five years: And Enoch walked with God: and he was not; for God took him" (Genesis 5:23-24).

Methuselah – 969 years
"And all the days of Methuselah were nine hundred sixty and nine years: and he died" (Genesis 5:27).

Lamech – 777 years
"And all the days of Lamech were seven hundred seventy and seven years: and he died" (Genesis 5:31).

Noah – 950 years
"And all the days of Noah were nine hundred and fifty years: and he died" (Genesis 9:29).

What is Health? - Student -

Second 10 Generations

Shem – 600 years
"These are the generations of Shem: Shem was an hundred years old, and begat Arphaxad two years after the flood:

"And Shem lived after he begat Arphaxad five hundred years, and begat sons and daughters" (Genesis 11:10-11).

Arphaxad – 438 years
"And Arphaxad lived five and thirty years, and begat Salah:

"And Arphaxad lived after be begat Salah four hundred and three years, and begat sons and daughters" (Genesis 11:12-13).

Salah – 433 years
"And Salah lived thirty years, and begat Eber:

"And Salah lived after he begat Eber four hundred and three years, and begat sons and daughters" (Genesis 11:14-15).

Eber – 464 years
"And Eber lived four and thirty years, and beat Peleg:

"And Eber lived after be begat Peleg four hundred and thirty years, and begat sons and daughters" (Genesis 11:16-17).

Peleg – 239 years
"And Peleg lived thirty years, and begat Reu:

"And Peleg lived after he begat Reu two hundred and nine years, and begat sons and daughters" (Genesis 11:18-19).

Reu – 239 years
"And Reu lived two and thirty years, and begat Serug:

"And Reu lived after he begat Serug two hundred and seven years, and begat Nahor" (Genesis 11:20-21).

Serug – 230 years
"And Serug lived thirty years, and begat sons and daughters.

"And Serug lived after he begat Nahor two hundred years, and begat sons and daughters" (Genesis 11:22-23).

Nahor – 148 years
"And Nahor lived nine and twenty years, and begat Terah:

"And Nahor lived after he begat Terah an hundred and nineteen years, and begat sons and daughters" (Genesis 11:24-25).

Terah – 205 years
"And Terah lived seventy years, and begat Abram, Nahor, and Haran.

"And the days of Terah were two hundred and five years: and Terah died in Haran" (Genesis 11:26, 32).

Abraham – 175 years
"And these are the days of the years of Abraham's life which he lived, an hundred threescore and fifteen years" (Genesis 25:7).

Today – 70 years
"The days of our years are threescore years and ten; and if by reason of strength they be fourscore years, yet is their strength labour and sorrow; for it is soon cut off, and we fly away" (Psalm 90:10).

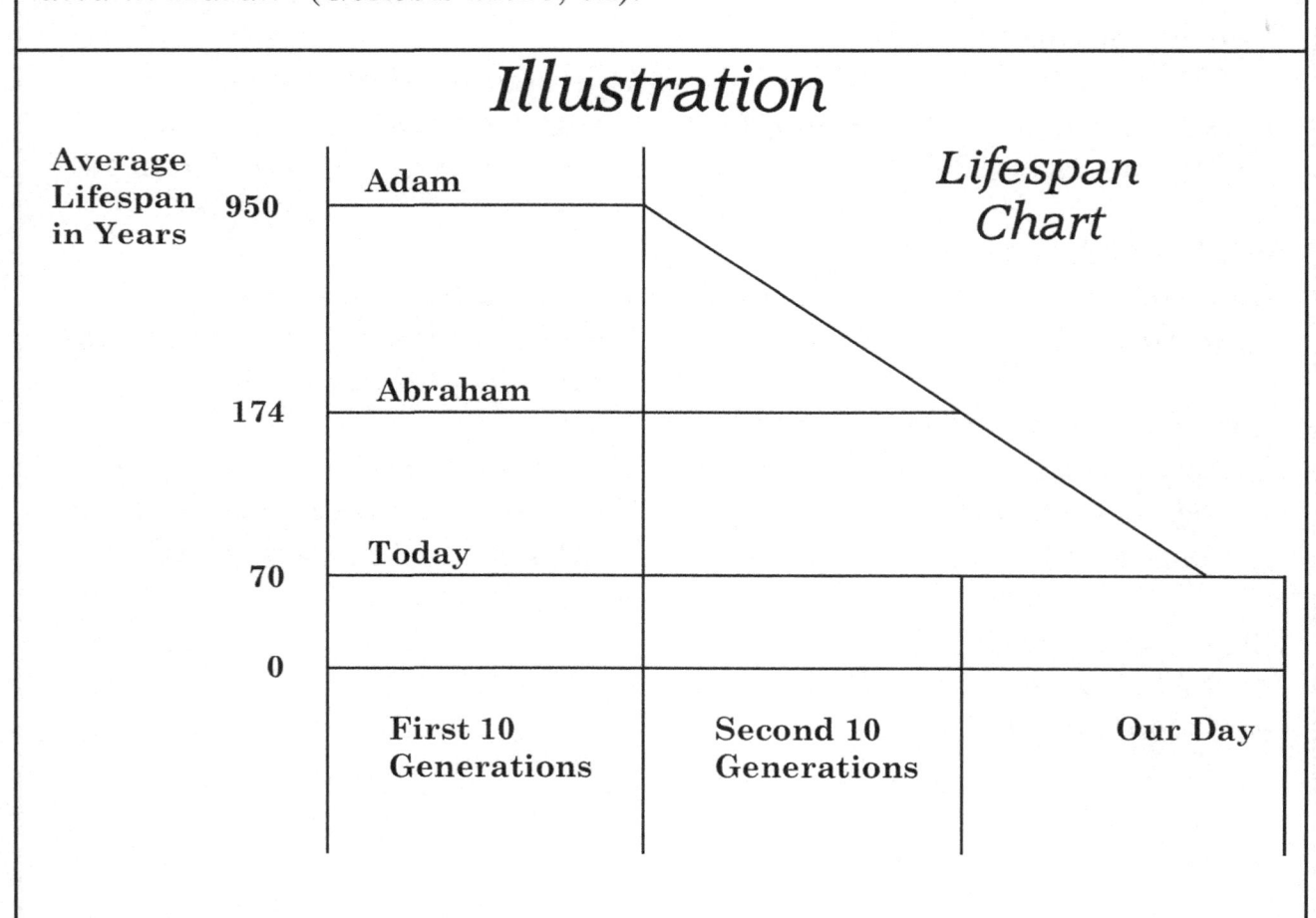

Illustration

Lifespan Chart

Average Lifespan in Years

Years	Generation
950	Adam
174	Abraham
70	Today
0	

First 10 Generations | Second 10 Generations | Our Day

What is Health? - Student - Page 48

When man follows God's plan, he will live a long, and happy life. Notice after ten generations from Adam to Noah, man lived about 950 years. Then from Shem to Abraham which was the second "ten generations," the lifespan dropped to only about 175 years. This is an eighty percent reduction which took place within only 526 years after the flood.

Perverted appetites and passions brought on the flood, and then added to this the eating of flesh foods, which accelerated body wear-and-tear and caused earlier death. So the first 10 generations (except Enoch) died of "old age." The second 10 generations died much younger.

First 10 Generations	Second 10 Generations
Adam – 930	Shem – 600 years
Seth – 912	Arphaxad – 438 years
Enos – 905	Salah – 433 years
Cainan – 910	Eber – 464 years
Mahalaleel – 895	Peleg – 239 years
Jared – 962	Reu – 239 years
Enoch – 365 (Translated)	Serug – 230 years
Methuselah – 969	Nahor – 148 years
Lamech – 777	Terah – 205 years
Noah – 950	Abraham – 175 years

Noah, the 10th generation, lived 20 years longer than Adam; the 8th generation lived 39 years longer than Adam; Shem lived to a fair age; but the 2nd generation after the flood dropped to 438 years; and the 8th generation, instead of being the longest as before the flood, was the shortest—only 148 years.

What is Health? - Student - Page 49

Vitality Summary

• We are given a certain amount of vitality or natural force.

• In **love**, God gives us enough vitality to recover from some transgressions of the laws of health.

• If we make a habit of wasting our vitality we can run out of it.

• When we run out of vitality the body gets seriously diseased and does not have the energy left to recover.

• If the Lord sees it is best, He may supernaturally impart His own life force to someone who is truly repentant about wasting his vitality.

Remind

1. When someone loses his or her temper because he or she runs out of patience, it can remind you of how disease appears when the body has run out of vital capital. Little transgressions add up to big problems.

2. When little sister is playing with blocks and the last one stacked on top wrongly causes the whole structure to fall down, be reminded of the physical parallel. One more small transgression on top of many others can result in death.

3. When sowing seeds in the garden think about what you are sowing in regard to your health. You will reap in your body the results of the habits you form in youth.

4. Putting money in your savings' bank can bring to mind the importance of building up your health so you will have the vital capital necessary to meet an emergency.

5. When someone puts too much wood all at once on a slow-burning fire it may start to smoke instead of burning fire. It is being smothered. This can remind you of the effects in the body from eating too much food at a meal. Neither the nutritive or the cleansing actions can be properly performed in this case. There is also a waste of vital capital.

What is Health? - Student -

Review

Place I - II - III

1. Vital capital is a certain amount of _____ _____ the organs have to use in case of _____.

2. What does "reserve" mean?

3. The Bible term for vital capital is _____ _____.

4. Are our organs capable of doing a lot more work than their ordinary share?

5. Why do people get the mistaken idea that they can continue to violate the laws of health and still recover?

Place III

6. What course would you advise someone to pursue who has wasted his vital capital?

7. What relation do little things have to diseases that last a long time (also called chronic diseases)?

8. What does Jeremiah 33:6 reveal about how a person recovers from a disease? What does it imply about the relationship of health to spiritual revelation?

9. One time when Christ healed disease, He warned the person *"Sin no more, lest a worse thing come unto thee"* (John 5:14). How does this text relate to what you have learned about vital capital?

Place I - Color the picture of the healed man.

What is Health? - Student - Page 51

A Sound Mind in a Sound Body

Most persons have heard this trite saying,
    And yielded a careless assent;
But few minds are suitably weighing
    The thought in its fullest extent.

It is known that a mortal contusion,*
    Or pressure extreme on the brain,
Will throw the mind into confusion,
    And render the person insane.

'Tis known that alcoholic drinks and narcotics
    Will prostrate both body and mind;
But yet there are other exotics,
    Whose evil is not so defined;

Whose death-work is not so alarming,
    But stealthily still it goes on;
More slowly but steadily harming
    The life-force until it is gone.

Few think that our eating and drinking,
    And habits of life every day,
Wield a mighty control o'er our thinking,
    Our tempers and passions to sway.

To think our religious devotion
    Affected by matters so small,
Is thought but a fanciful notion,
    Deserving no credit at all.

*bad injury caused by a blow

But yet, in great measure, our mental,
    Depends on our bodily state;
And this not a thing accidental,
    But governed by laws wise and great.

Transgressing the laws of our being
    Beclouds and debases the mind,
Prevents us from morally seeing
    And makes us to law disinclined.

As you prize then a clear moral vision,
    No longer the good work delay;
But come to the faithful decision
    To break your false habits today.

Treat the body according to reason,
    And reason will dawn in the mind;
Begin the good work now in season,
    And the truth of our motto you'll find.

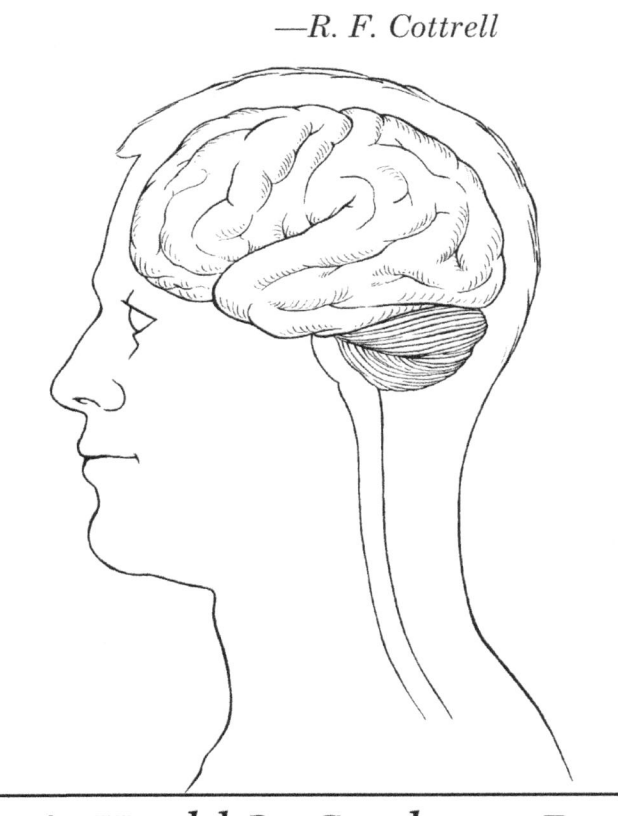

—R. F. Cottrell

Research
Conditions of Cure

"My son, attend to my words; For they are life unto those that find them, and health to all their flesh."
Proverbs 4:20, 22

In **love**, God gave the Israelites definite instructions in regard to their habits of life. He made known to them the laws relating to both physical and spiritual well-being; and on condition of obedience He **lovingly** assured them, *"the Lord will take away from thee all sickness"* (Deuteronomy 7:15). *"Set your hearts unto all the words which I testify among you this day." "For they are life unto those that find them, and health to all their flesh"* (Deuteronomy 32:46; Proverbs 4:22).

God's **loving** dealings with the Israelites in the Old Testament have been recorded *"for our learning"* (Romans 15:4). God promised them, *"If thou wilt diligently hearken to the voice of the LORD thy God, and wilt do that which is right in his sight, and wilt give ear to his commandments, and keep all his statutes, I will put none of these diseases upon thee, which I have brought upon the Egyptians: for I am the LORD that healeth thee"* (Exodus 15:26). The word Lord in this text is Yahweh (Rophe-ka) which means "the Lord thy Physician."

There are three important points in this promise. First, God gives this promise of healing upon certain conditions. That is why He uses the word *"if."* The healing depends upon doing what God asks. Second, the promise is made to individuals. That means that everyone, man, woman, or child, is required to carry out what God says is necessary to healing. Third, the people had to make a habit of doing what God said. It could not be an on and off affair. They must *"diligently"* work at it every day. The result of cooperating with God's conditions is freedom from disease. Since Jesus Christ is *"the same yesterday, and to day, and for ever,"* He makes the same promise to His children today based upon the same conditions.

The Lord is the Great Physician

What is Health? - Student - Page 54

The four things God requires are:

1. *"If thou wilt diligently hearken to the voice of the Lord thy God"*

2. If *"thou...wilt do that which is right in his sight"*

3. If thou *"wilt give ear to his commandments"*

4. If *"thou...wilt keep all his statutes"*

Numbers 1 and 3 show the need for listening carefully to exactly what God requires. Numbers 2 and 4 put the emphasis on obedience to each **loving** detail. They tell us that if we will *"do"* and *"keep"* then God will do His part of the promise to restore us to health.

Those whose minds and bodies are diseased are to behold Christ the Restorer. *"Because I live"* He says, *"ye shall live also"* (John 14:19). This is the life we are to **lovingly** present to the sick. Tell them that if they have faith in Christ as the Restorer, if they cooperate with Him, obeying the laws of health, He will supernaturally give them His own life.

Jesus is our Great Physician and He is a specialist in every area for He *"healeth all thy diseases"* (Psalm 103:3).

Reinforce

Sing the hymn, "The Great Physician."

The Goal

God calls upon us to make our choices on the right side, to connect with heavenly agencies, to adopt principles that will completely restore in us the divine image. In His written word and in the great book of nature He has revealed the principles of life. It is our work to obtain a knowledge of these principles, and by obedience to cooperate with Him in restoring health to the body as well as to the soul.

Grace is Needed

"That ye may be blameless and harmless, the sons of God, without rebuke, in the midst of a crooked and perverse nation, among whom ye shine as lights in the world."
Philippians 2:15

To learn about the laws of health and how to live is not enough. We must have the power to obey these laws. The blessings of obedience can be ours only as we receive the grace of Christ. God's free grace is the desire and the power to do His will. It is God's grace that gives people the power to obey God's law of **love**, including the **loving** laws of health. It is this that enables people to break the bondage of evil habits. This is the only power that can make and keep us steadfast in the right path.

Reinforce

Explain what Philippians 2:15 and I Corinthians 15:10 mean.

Color the picture.

*"But by the grace of God
I am what I am:
and his grace which was
bestowed upon me
was not in vain;
but I labored
more abundantly
than they all: yet not I,
but the grace of God
which was with me."*
I Corinthians 15:10

*Animals
more readily obey the laws
of their being than man does.*

Sing This Song

THE GREAT PHYSICIAN

William Hunter
Arr. J. H. Stockton

1. The great Phys-i-cian now is near, The sym-pa-thiz-ing Je-sus;
2. Your man-y sins are all for-giv'n, O hear the voice of Je-sus;
3. All glo-ry to the dy-ing Lamb! I now be-lieve in Je-sus;
4. His name dis-pels my guilt and fear; No oth-er name but Je-sus;
5. And when He comes to bring the crown,— The crown of life and glo-ry;

He speaks, the droop-ing heart to cheer, O hear the voice of Je-sus!
Go on your way in peace to heav'n, And wear a crown with Je-sus.
I love the bless-ed Sav-iour's name, I love the name of Je-sus.
O how my soul de-lights to hear The pre-cious name of Je-sus!
Then by His side we will sit down, And tell re-demp-tion's sto-ry.

Chorus

Sweet-est note in ser-aph song, Sweet-est name on mor-tal tongue,
Sweet-est car-ol ev-er sung,— Je-sus, bless-ed Je-sus!

Reinforce
Place II - III

Place the underlined words in this crossword.

<u>When</u> <u>He</u> <u>was</u> <u>upon</u> <u>earth</u>, <u>the</u> <u>Great</u> <u>Physician</u>, <u>Jesus</u> <u>Christ</u>, <u>never</u> <u>lost</u> a <u>case</u>.

"...<u>Great</u> <u>multitudes</u> <u>followed</u> <u>him</u>, and he <u>healed</u> <u>them</u> <u>all</u>."
(Matthew 12:15)

What is Health? - Student - Page 58

Reinforce
Place I

Color these words and read them to your teacher.

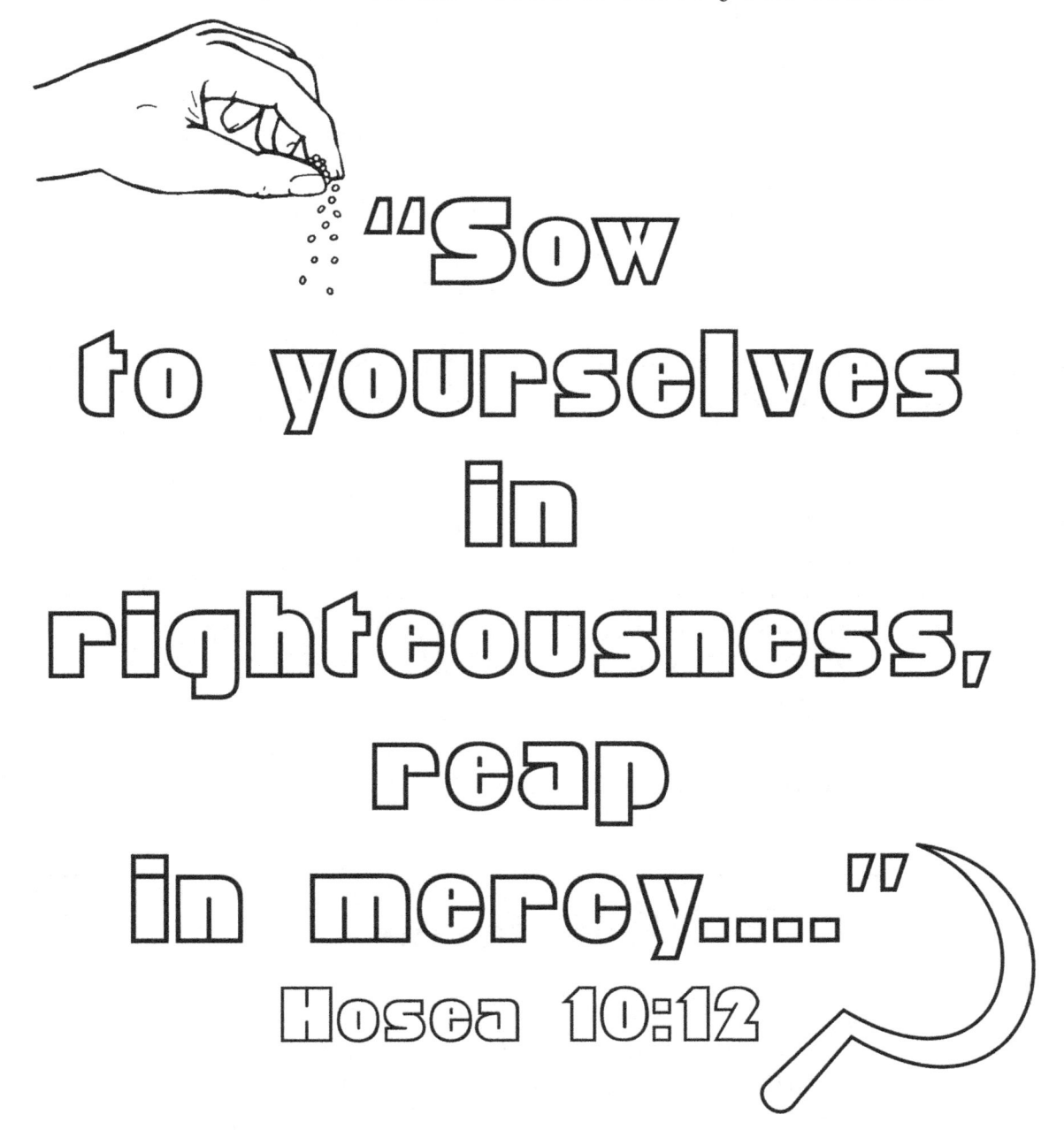

"Sow to yourselves in righteousness, reap in mercy...."
Hosea 10:12

What is Health? - Student - Page 59

Bible Search
Physical Healing

1. What part did Abraham play in the healing of Abimelech and his wife? (Genesis 20:17)

2. What natural remedy did the prophet Elisha prescribe for Naaman's leprosy? (II Kings 5:1-19)

3. What kind of prayer is needed in the case of the sick? (James 5:13-16)

4. Who was the king that was cured of a terminal* illness by prayer, confession of sin, and using a divinely prescribed natural remedy? (II Kings 20:1-7) What was the natural remedy?

5. What agency did God use to bring healing in Psalm 107:20?

6. Memorize the prayer found in Psalm 41:1-4.

7. How does rebellion against God affect the whole body? (Isaiah 1:5-20)

8. Whose ministry among God's faithful workers did He allow to be held up by illness? (II Timothy 4:20; and Philippians 2:25-30)

Reinforce

Read the following story,
"Some Chapters of Bob's Early Life."
Then carefully answer the questions at the end pertaining
to the laws of health that were violated,
and the character quality of **love**.

*the end of something

What is Health? - Student - Page 60

Some Chapters of Bob's Early Life

I. An Early Abstinence Movement

II. "Mere Bits O' Brass"

III. Fingers and Toes

IV. Trying

V. Success and Trial

VI. Conclusion

I. An Early Abstinence* Movement

In the year 1842 the abstinence movement* was new and much looked down upon. And it was therefore not without opposition that some friends and myself were permitted to start a society in the mission district of the church to which we belonged. We had church services for grown-up people, and at last, in addition, this abstinence society.

In order to stir up an interest in our new movement, and also to silence the sneer of those who said that no good would come of it, we resolved to have a house-to-house visitation of the district, and invite the people personally to our first meeting. It was while carrying out this part of our plan that we first met with "Bob," the story of whose early life I am about to tell.

The mission district was a street, from which long and crowded courts, opened on either side, and went so far back that they were narrow streets themselves. And, indeed, each of these courts was a world in itself. In one of the most open of them was a great stretch of brick wall, enclosing a slater's** yard. And this wall we found all chalked over with sketches of dogs' and horses' heads. Struck by the power and beauty of these, we inquired who the artist was. But the only reply we could get was— "Oh, it'll be Bob;" or, "Oh, no doubt it's some of Bob's nonsense;" or something to that effect. One thing only was clear, that the artist's name in the district was "Bob."

We might never have known more than that, if we had not carried out our house-to-house visitation. But in the course of our visiting we came across Bob himself. We found him to be a young lad about seventeen—tall, fair, blue-eyed, with hair tossed back in a mass over his brow, and with a soft and pleasant voice. He was living with his mother in a small "room and kitchen" house, and was sitting at a table when we entered, drawing some figures on a slate. Entering into conversation with his mother and him, we found them ready to join our society; and, in fact, before we left the house the young lad had consented to be a sort of district secretary of the movement.

Before two days were over, we had a very effective proof that our new secretary was in earnest. The sketches of dogs' and horses' heads

---

*This was especially for the purpose of warning people about the use of alcoholic beverages.
**one that lays slates (stones which readily split into plates), or whose job is to slate buildings

were all rubbed out, and a real temperance picture chalked over the slateyard wall. At one end was a great whisky-barrel, with open doors like a shop, and a stream of people issuing out into the street. Beggars, thieves, fallen women, drunken workmen, drunken masters, drunkards of every age and class made up this procession. At the other end of the wall was a gallows, and at its foot a lot of dead people huddled in a heap. The picture was very rude—as rude and bald as a picture could well be—but the meaning was pretty clear on the whole, and it was made plain to everybody by the words below—"What comes out of the whisky-barrel." Along the top of the wall there ran an announcement of our meeting.

The meeting was a great success. But we were much indebted for that to Bob's chalk drawing. His mother and he were among the first to arrive, and by-and-by our little hall was full.

The speaking was not very bright. We were all beginners in the work, and we had none of the facts at our finger tips which make it easy to fill a temperance speech now. But we did our best, and we got some of the people themselves to say a word or two; and what was better than all, and quite unlooked for, we got a speech from Bob.

It came about in this way. We were proposing some votes of thanks at the close, and one of us rose and said the greatest thanks were due to the artist who helped us by his temperance picture. The meeting caught up the idea at once, and over the whole meeting rose loud cries for Bob, and clapping of hands. Bob's face went very red; but the people were resolved he should rise. And at last, after we also had pressed him strongly, he got up and spoke something to this effect:

"I am not a great drawer: but I can draw better than I can speak. But I can say this much, that it's a good work we've begun this night. It's the work of putting down drinking and saving drinkers and we can all help in this work if we only keep away from drink ourselves.

"I believe the work will succeed. I hope every lad and lass here will put down their names. I am going to put down mine. Not that the putting down of our names will make us sober,—but it'll show what side we're on. And it'll help to keep us away from drink. We can all say, if we're asked to drink, 'I've put down my name.' That's all I have to say."

II. "Mere Bits O' Brass"

Bob was little more than seventeen when these events took place. But the story I am going to tell begins seven years before. He was at that time a small piecer in a cotton factory, and his mother was an outdoor worker for the same. The mother's occupation was "reeling." She had a long wooden reel in her house, on which she wound hanks of yarn. At this work she made about five shillings a week. Bob got two. This was all their living.

At that time they lived, not in the house where I first saw them, but in a miserable single apartment in the very roof of a four-story building. It was a poor, cold, wretched little place. There was a tiny window in the gable of the roof, and a fireplace as tiny beside it. The reel filled one side of the room, the two beds in which Bob and his mother slept, left hardly room to move between. I never heard who Bob's father was, or whether he was living, or dead, or anything at all about him. And those who knew Bob and his mother most intimately knew as little as I.

In the humble attic which I have described, this poor place, hot in summer and cold in winter, lived Bob and his mother,— Bell was her Christian name—in the year 1835, when my story begins. In the winter evenings, when the rain was lashing on the slates overhead and sometimes dropping through, Bell and her piecer-boy would draw near the mite of a fireplace, poke the handful of coals in the grate into a glow to save a candle, draw the three-legged stool between them, and take their morsel of supper all alone. And poor though they were, those were happy times for these two—and times they often looked back to with tears in their eyes in the dark days near at hand.

At that time children as young as Bob were allowed to work in factories. And the two shillings a-week which he earned was a great addition to his mother's means. His work was to walk backward and forward with the spinning-jenny and piece up threads which broke, and now and again to creep below the machine and sweep the cotton dust from the floor. It was not hard work, nor very dangerous; and if the spinner happened to be a kindly man, children could be very happy at the work. But ten years of age was very young even in those days. And it was an age when an innocent and unsuspecting child might very easily be tempted into crime.

At the machine next to the one where Bob "pieced" was a boy two years older, called Ned. Now Ned had not even a mother to **love** and care for him, or tell him what was good or bad. And being but a boy, and not having been taught to **love** anything better, Ned set his heart on sweets. "Candy," "white rock," "shortbread," and etc. were the things in the world which Ned thought best worth having. But he had only two and sixpence a-week, and it took all that, and what the parish allowed besides, to pay for Ned's lodging and keep. Ned had once or twice in his life had a penny, and he always spent it on sweets. And now he set his heart on having sweets. Ned fell into a snare that is very common in this world. He fell into the snare of *"hasting to be rich"* (Proverbs 28:20). He said to himself—"It will be a long while before I can earn as much as will let me buy sweets for myself. But if I had some of these brass things lying about, I could get as much as ever I wanted." But he could not get brass things which were not his own without help. So he walked home with Bob every night for a week, and, bit by bit, told him of the joys of eating sweets, and of the easy way by which they could get as much of these as they liked—"We've only to take a ball socket or two. And Bob, they're useless things—mere bits o' brass—they'll never be missed."

I am telling the story just as it happened. I do not wish to make Ned out a villain and Bob an innocent victim. It is true, Ned was older, and he was the tempter; but Bob knew things that Ned never heard of, and yet he let himself be tempted. He knew well enough it was stealing to which Ned was coaxing him. And it was the work of a thief they two agreed to do.

The articles they stole were things which boys might well fancy were only worth as old brass— "Mere bits of brass"—as Ned said. They were spare fittings kept lying about to be ready for use. And the boys easily found a wicked storekeeper outside to give them pennies for each article they brought. It was some time before the fittings were missed. But after the thefts had gone on for several weeks the number of things missed became so great, that the whole factory got into a stir to find out the thieves. In this the men were as earnest as the masters, and suggested a plan by which the thief might be found out.

It was noticed that the thefts were mostly on a certain day of the week when the factory closed at four. On one of these days, as the work people came down into the court, they found two policemen stationed at the door, who searched each individual as he stepped out.

What Is Health? - Student - Page 65

Then each stood aside to see their neighbors searched. By-and-by Ned and Bob, suspecting nothing, came out with the usual bit of brass in a sleeve of their jackets, and were discovered at once. Their first taste of the evil of crime was the sharp clutch the policemen took of their arms, and the howl of anger which rose up from the crowd, who had waited to the end.

I do not know what happened in Ned's lodging that evening. But in the lone attic where Bell waited to give her boy his supper, what took place was worse than death. Two policemen and one of the factory foremen came up and searched every corner of the room, and although nothing was found, she was told in a cruel way of her boy's guilt, and informed that she could have no more work from the mill.

Poor, lonely, innocent Bell! Her sorrow was too great for tears. It seemed as if her heart would burst. At first she was stunned. Then she became excited. Then she started from her seat, and paced up and down the little attic till far into the night. Then she lay down, but could not sleep. The two thoughts which chased each other through her soul were—"My boy a thief! My boy in jail!" On the next morning she tried to think it was all a dream, and that Bob had only been out all night. And then she listened to noises below as if these might be his foot on the stair. She never seemed to have thought of going to see him in the jail. She was not herself. As the hours of that day went on she still listened for his step on the stair. She neither lit her fire nor took food all that day; and it was the end of December, and bitterly cold. What was heat or cold, or food or hunger to the **loving** mother whose only child was in jail?

III. Fingers and Toes

Daylight drearily dawned that next morning in the poor attic where Bell had passed another miserable night. She knew that her boy would be brought before the magistrates that morning, and wrapping her thin blue mantle around her, and drawing its hood over her head, she tottered rather than walked—shrinking from the gaze of every passer-by—to the court where he was to appear.

She had not long to wait; Ned and he were brought up among the first. It was no bad dream she had dreamed. That was her own boy, her one delight on earth, whom she beheld in the dock. But could it all be true? Had the harsh policemen not made matters worse than they were? Could so young a child have done all the evil they said? Could he have gone on doing it, and she not know? Perhaps, after all, her boy was innocent; perhaps somebody would step out of the crowd and say he was innocent. Alas! Ned and he had been taken in the very act, and they did not once try to deny their crime.

They had really stolen the bits of brass; they had been stealing them for many weeks. The poor children cried the whole time of the trial. At the close, each got sixty days in prison.

As the two boys were marched out of the court, Bell fairly broke down, and had to be helped into the street.

It was December when this took place. Winter had set in early that season, and was very severe. A long-continued and hard frost lay upon the land, and great suffering fell even upon those who were free among the people. The suffering was still greater in the prisons. No **loving** tenderness has come to human hearts then on behalf of prisoners. No one thought their health worth caring for. The prison cell was not heated; the bed-coverings were scant; the food was poor. And the frost struck through with all its might at the two pitiful children who were shut up in a dismal cell. Bob suffered the most; he was of a fragile make. He had never been very strong, and long before the sixty days had come to a close, his naked feet were bitten with the frost, and two of his toes ready to drop off.

At last, however, came the long-wearied-for sixtieth day when the poor children were to be let free.

What Is Health? - Student - Page 67

Poor Bob! The day of his freedom was a day of sorrow. It was a cold raw February day, a bitter east wind blowing along the street, and the pavement with the slush of snow that had fallen the night before. About a dozen prisoners were to be let out that morning, and a crowd of poor people who expected them were gathered about the gate. One here, and another there, gave a joyful cry as they got back some member of their circle. Bob had thought that his mother would be surely there. He had often wondered why she had not come to see him, but the thought that he should meet her now had kept him awake the only part of the night when the pain in his foot was quiet enough to let him sleep He looked eagerly around, but she was nowhere in the crowd, and tears came into his eyes as he edged side-ways from the throng and began to limp towards his old home. It was slow work. He could only put the heel of his disabled foot to the ground, and to do even that much was painful. Often he rested by the way. Then pains of another kind shot through his heart. As he came near the court where he was so well known, and in which he had gained so early an evil reputation, shame took hold upon him. He was afraid to be seen; afraid that people would reproach him; afraid that his mother would never **love** him again; but afraid most of all, perhaps, lest he should meet the policemen who had taken him first to prison.

At length he was at the foot of the long "turn-pike" stair that led up to his mother's attic. The pain in going up the steps was terrible. Several times he had to sit down and rest. At the last flight of steps he had to crawl on hands and knees. He began to be terribly shaken and afraid. As he crawled upwards he heard no sound; the stillness was like the grave. When he came to the door his strength was utterly gone. He could not reach up to the latch. "Mother," he cried; but no **loving** mother appeared. He knocked, but there was no answer. Struggling up in a last effort of strength to the latch, he tried to open the door; it was locked. He sunk down on the threshold and sobbed aloud. He must have lain huddled up in that state for some hours, and fallen asleep. What he next remembered was the confusion of voices at the foot of the stairs.

"Somebody's moaning at Bell's door."

"What did you say? What can it be?"

"Has she maybe died in the hospital?"

And then Bob saw the heads of four or five neighboring women peering up at him from the stair. "Oh, me," said one of them, "it's Bob." "I declare it's Bell's laddie come again!" And the same voice added, "O laddie, laddie, you have done much mischief. Your mother's in the hospital with the fever."

When he came to himself he was on a shake-down in the warm kitchen of one of the houses on the landing below. I will give the name of the **loving** Samaritan who took him in. It was Mrs. Greenwood, the Lady Bountiful of that little world, the kind-hearted wife of a kind-hearted man. When the two heard that the boy was home and ill, they opened their door and "took him in."

Bob never forgot the **loving** kindness received from these two that night. It was the nearest approach to Heaven he had ever known. It was a kindness that did not work by halves; they kept the boy till his mother was better, and back in her home.

What Is Health? - Student - Page 69

IV. Trying

It was a long while before Bob was able to walk, and when he got out again it was with eight toes instead of ten. That was a terrible infliction for his mother and him. It was loss of bread. The mill district of the city at that time was little better than a village. Everybody knew everybody else. And Bell and her boy were only too well known. The toes were a sort of Cain's mark on the boy—a certificate of conduct telling the wrong way. He was too poor to have shoes. The toes told of prison; and prison brought back the story of the bits of brass. And factory after factory refused to receive him within their gates.

By the help of some neighbors, Bell got work for her reel; but she was no longer able for the amount of work she could do before her illness; and the want of Bob's wages made a great difference in her means.

But God was kind. Gifts of love from unknown givers came to them in the form of coal and potatoes and meal. Bob was able now and again to gain a penny by holding horses on market days, and running messages. And the Greenwoods remained fast friends to him till his troubles were over.

Although Mr. Greenwood lived in a humble situation, he was a man of some wealth. He lived behind his clothier's shop that fronted the street. This was a main resort for Bob; and he was always made welcome there. Mr. Greenwood saw that the boy had learned by what he had suffered; and that he was turned away from dishonest ways for ever. He believed in the boy and trusted him, and thought up many a message just to give Bob the pleasure of earning an honest penny. But he did more than that. He encouraged the boy to spend his leisure time in learning. And sitting at the friendly fire in the cutting-room, Bob learned to be a thoroughly good reader, and found out that he had a gift for drawing. There was a slate in the shop on which many a rude drawing was made with the fine chalk used by clothiers. And the kindly man would stop his work to admire a face, or a tree, or a bridge, when the boy tried to draw these objects on the slate.

One morning the clothier was sitting on his bench reading the weekly paper as Bob came in. "Bob," he said, "I see something in the paper this morning that will do for you." It was an advertisement by a great pattern-designing and art publishing firm for an apprentice. "Look here, Bob," the eager friend said, "the only condition is, that the boy must have a taste for drawing."

But Bob replied: "They will look at my toes." "No;" said Mr. Greenwood, "and don't you say anything about your toes. And nobody now has any business to ask you about the past. You have suffered plenty already by these toes. At any rate, you go and try; and go this very forenoon.

Bob returned home and told his mother. He was made as tidy and clean as possible. And looking in as he passed at his friend's shop, the boy set off.

He knew the building well at whose door he had to knock. Often he had passed it when delivering messages. Often had he looked in the winter evenings at its three tiers of windows all lighted up. Often on such evenings had he marked the flitting shadows of the printers as they moved among the presses. Often he had been struck in the daytime with the great rope dangling from the topmost story at one end and swinging up and down great bales of paper. Oftener still, he had stopped for a moment at the beautiful porch at the other end, and looked through the glass door at the fine pictures and statues which were ranged around the walls of the entrance hall. At this very door he stood this morning, but with fear filling his heart. What chance had he, so poor, so ragged, to be received in a place so fine?

And, indeed, he seemed very poor. No wonder the junior partner, Mr. Bathgate, looked at him as he was shown into his room. He was still a tiny-looking boy—he had not begun yet to shoot up into the tall youth he had become when we first met with him. And he was barefooted. And his trousers, through honest wear, were more like knickerbockers than trousers. His jacket also was too small for him. The cap he held in his hand was not without a hole or two. But over against all this, there was an intelligent face, two honest eyes, hair combed beautifully to one side, and hands and legs and face as clean as water could make them.

This was the conversation which followed:—

"You want to become our apprentice, my little man?"

"Yes sir."

"Can you draw?"

"A little bit."

"What can you draw?"

"Dogs and horses and trees."

"Who taught you?"

"Myself."

"Well, take this home with you, and let me see what sort of copy you can make of it."

Mr. Bathgate took a wood-engraved landscape from a desk, a sheet of cardboard, and a pencil, wrapped them up for the boy, and told him to come back when he had made a copy.

Whoever saw Bob that forenoon as he turned his steps towards his home, saw a boy who ran as if he had wings. He seemed to himself to have become suddenly the heir of a great possession. The sheet of cardboard, the new pencil, the fine engraving; he had never had such things in his hand before. He did not stop till he reached his patron's shop, and unrolled his treasure on his cutting board. But Mr. Greenwood's heart gave way a little when he saw the landscape. "Can you manage this, do you think, Bob?" "I'll try," said Bob. And away he ran up the long stairs to his mother.

He heard the reel as he came up the stair. There she was, when the boy pushed open the door—winding, winding, winding. The only events of her life were going to the mill for copes, and returning with hanks—and, besides that, seeing her boy come in at the door. Today he was unlike what she had ever seen him. He seemed to have grown taller. His face was filled with eager hope. He was panting to tell her what had taken place. But he had also a great favor to ask. "Mother, could you give me a penny?" (Do not smile you to whom a penny is nothing.) "A penny, Bob?" "Yes, mother—to get a penny candle. I'll have to sit up a while after you've been to bed." Bob got the penny, changed that for a candle, and at once settled down to his task.

He had a good many hours yet of daylight, and he used them well. He had never worked with so soft a pencil, or on paper so fit for drawing. And he worked with great care. Then, when evening came on, he lit his candle and still continued to work. His mother went to bed; but Bob worked on. He heard the cuckoo-clock in the house below striking the hours till far into the morning. About four o'clock he laid down his pencil. The task was done. Then he **lovingly** set the fire for his mother's breakfast, put the kettle near, and slipped into bed.

At ten o'clock he was at Mr. Bathgate's office door.

"What!" said that gentleman, "are you back again? The work has been too hard for you, I fear."

"No."

"But you can't have done it already."

"Yes sir; it's here."

"This! Did you do this? You? Yourself? When did you do it?"

"I sat up all night till I finished it."

"Did you though? Sat up till you did it?"

Just then Mr. Currie, the other partner, came in; and the two went into an inner room and had a long examination of the copy. It had been beautifully done. At last coming back into the room where Bob was, they said,—

"We are very much pleased with the copy you have made. You would make a capital designer. But we are afraid our place will hardly suit you." Bob's heart sank.

"We give no wages to our apprentices; and our apprentices have to pay us for teaching them."

There was a little quiver on the boy's lips as he answered, "But I must have wages; I must try to help my mother now."

The two partners looked at each other for a moment, and went into the inner room again. In a short time one of them came out and said,—"Come back here on Monday, and we'll think over your application till then."

When Bob returned on Monday, he was told they were so much pleased with the copy he had drawn, that they had resolved to make an exception in his favor. They would take him without a premium, and they would give him three shillings and sixpence a week the first year of his apprenticeship. He might begin next day.

That was a day of joy in the little world where the principal people were the Greenwoods, and Bell, and her boy. Mr. Greenwood rigged up the boy in a new suit of clothes, which he could pay for when he was rich. He got his neighbor the shoemaker to give a pair of shoes on the same terms. And Bob's career began.

V. Success and Trial

Bob succeeded beyond all expectation. He became one of the best designers and draughtsmen in the establishment. At the end of two years he was receiving ten shillings a week, and able to take a better house for his mother. And long before the seven years of his apprenticeship were finished, he was the most trusted man in the place, and the one to whom a difficult piece of work was certain to be sent. When his time was over, the partners marked their satisfaction with him by making him a gift of money and a beautiful watch, and at the same time appointing him manager over a special department of their work.

But Bob was not to enter on his new kingdom without both trial and sorrow. It was at that time a universal custom in workshops and warehouses for workmen to give "treats" of alcoholic beverages on all the great occasions of their career. There was the " 'prentice pint," the "journeyman pint," and the "foreman pint." Bob's poverty had excused him from the first. But when he became journeyman and manager at one step, his fellow workmen demanded a special treat.

But Bob had, long before this, been drawn into our abstinence work. He was the secretary of our district society, and about to be made president. He was the leading spirit of our movement, and in thorough earnest. And he flatly refused to give the treat demanded. Great offence was taken. I can look back to those times and vividly recall them. Not designers and printers only, but even some "ministers" of the gospel as well, were expected to give these "treats." A young minister coming into a Presbytery had to give a bottle of wine; and whether he drank or not, he had to pay his share of what others drank at the Presbytery dinners. It is difficult to believe now that anger so deep and bitter could be cherished towards the men who had the courage to refuse such demands. This anger came out in full strength, and over all the works, against Bob. "What! was he to set up to be better than his neighbors? Were the back-books of his life so clean that he set up to be the sober man of the works? It was mean. It was miserly. Only a sneak and a churl would act in that way." And Bob saw in the averted looks and short snappish answers he got, and in the sneery laughter of the workmen when he had occasion to pass, how greatly he had offended them.

One morning when he came to his desk he found a drawing of a right foot with only three toes on it. That was the morning of the day he came to my lodgings and told me of his sorrows, with tears in his eyes.

But there was worse to follow.

The evil customs which prevailed among work-people had companion customs among the masters. Bargains were made and accounts settled in the bar—and when it was not there, it was in the private parlor of the office, over wine and spirits. The latter was looked upon as the gentler way. And this was the way the great art-printing and publishing house of Currie & Bathgate did.

Now Bob's new position gave him a room in the premises which led into the private parlor. The ingenious malice of his enemies resolved to strike him in his most tender part. One forenoon, when Mr. Bathgate entered the private parlor with a customer, he found the cupboard in which the wines were kept had been tampered with, and a bottle of the rarest taken away. Nothing was said that day; but the same thing was noticed a few days later by Mr. Currie.

Before long several bottles were taken. Now nobody could enter this parlor by day unobserved by Bob. And nobody could so easily get access to the wine as he. But to do his masters justice, they never once suspected him. Here the malice of his enemies was completely at fault. They had planned their wickedness so that suspicion should fall on their victim. But their victim's character was now a divine shield around him.

Still the thefts went on, and began to be talked about among the men. The heads of the firm resolved to sift the matter to the bottom. Mr. Bathgate sent for Bob one afternoon into the private parlor, and laid a slip of paper before him on which these words were written: "Search the young foreman's room, you will find the bottles there." And the bottles were actually all found there that afternoon. "Now, Robert," said the friendly master, "This is a plot to hurt you. But it is also a wickedness which must not be permitted in our works. Whoever is the doer of it must work by night, for if it were done by day you must have found it out. Give me the key of your room for a night or two, and I will set a watch myself."

Robert was in the act of thanking his master for his good opinion of him, and was handing over his key, when the night porter knocked at the door. A great hamper had been delivered in the yard, and there was some living creature in it. Along with the hamper came a letter. It was from Mr. Bathgate's brother, the captain of a vessel trading to North America. He had been asked to bring a bear over to some zoological garden. He had no convenience to keep it in the ship after the men had left. Could his brother get it chained up in his yard for a night or two, till it could be sent off to its destination?

With great ado the bear was taken to the yard at the other end of the warehouse, and fastened up by its chain. More than an hour was spent over this business, and Bob and his master parted for the night.

It was a very eventful night for him. His enemies had resolved to complete his shame that night. The wine press was to be opened once more and a bottle broken, and its contents spilled over the floor of Bob's room. The young foreman's office-coat was to be dipped in the spilt wine, and to crown all, the skeleton key by which the press was opened was to be slipped into its pocket.

All this was done, and all this was discovered by Mr. Bathgate in the morning when he entered the room. He came early, before the bell had rung. A single glance sufficed to show him how matters stood. What he saw had been carefully planned; but those who planned it had never calculated that the masters would take the foreman's side. Was it conspiracy? Was it the work of only one? But how could any one have done what he saw? He was himself the last to leave the building. He had seen even the porter leave before him, and he was the first to arrive in the morning. A little while after came the porter, and began to light up the corridors and printing-rooms. By-and-by the various workpeople arrived. Mr. Bathgate, completely puzzled, was waiting in his office, wondering what next step should be taken to find out the culprit, when the porter rushed in, under great excitement, and told him that the bear had nearly killed a man. And sure enough, when they went to the yard in which the bear was chained, they saw a form huddled up in a corner and moaning between fear and pain. And they found the bear in a great rage, stretched to the full length of his chain, and pawing at the crouching form to get it into its grasp.

In this strange way the mystery was laid bare. The workman who had been detailed by those in the plot to bring Bob into trouble had hidden himself in the top story of the building, and after the mischief already described was wrought, had gone, as he had done night after night before, to the rope used for swinging up and down the bales of paper, to slide himself down into the yard, from whence, by climbing the wall, he could get away unperceived.

But the bear was an unexpected actor on the scene, and not until the miserable wretch was near the lower end of the rope did he become aware of its presence. Then he heard its breathing, then a harsh grunt or two, and before he could escape he was in the arms of this terrible creature. It would have been a relief to him to have known that it was a bear; he thought it was something infinitely worse. In his mortal terror he got loose from its first embrace, but the yard was too little for him to escape entirely. He could not get near the wall over which he expected to climb. It was to that wall the bear was chained. He could only dodge about in the opposite corners to escape the clutches of his dark-looking enemy. This unequal battle had lasted the whole night long. At last, completely cowed and prostrate, he gave in , and was found more dead than alive crouched up in a corner of the yard.

I need not dwell on what followed. The half-dozen who had plotted the mischief were dismissed. And Bob found himself higher in the esteem of his masters, and at last of his fellow workmen as well, than before. The affair led to another result that was good – the firm closed the wine parlor, and were among the first in the city to give up the practice of treating their customers to alcohol.

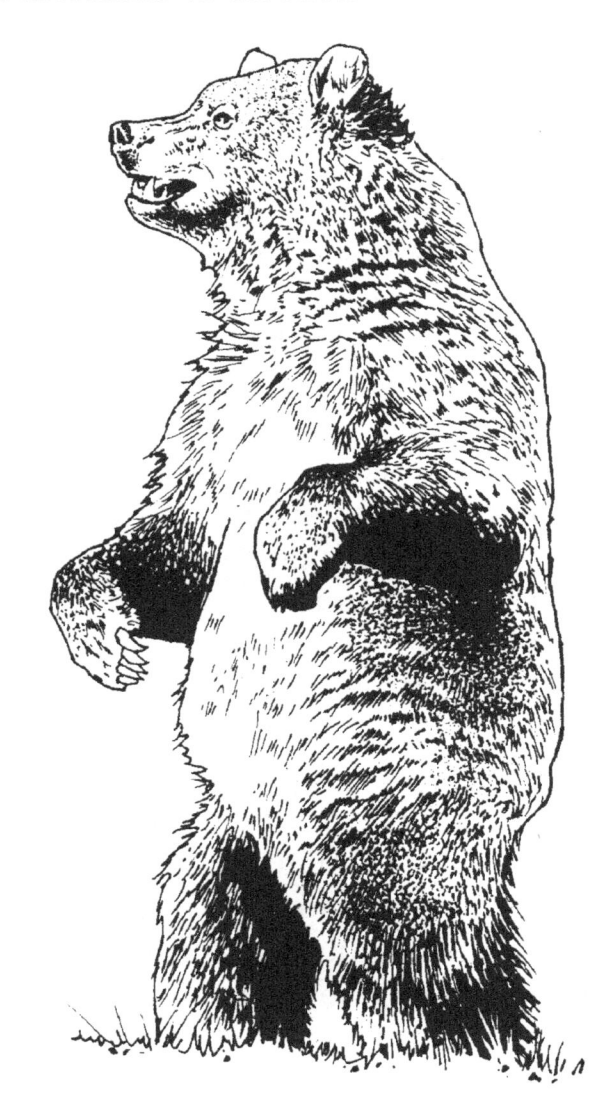

VI. Conclusion

Bob's next advance was Paris. The firm sent him there to study the designs of the Continent, and adapt them for English goods. The ragged boy who began at three shillings and sixpence a week was now a well-dressed, thoroughly educated artist, with a salary of three hundred pounds; and so well did he acquit himself in his new sphere that at the end of a few years he was asked to join the firm, and open a branch of their house in London.

Although he changed in many things, there was no change in his **love** for his mother. He was her stay and comfort as long as she lived. His respect for her was very beautiful. He bought a cottage for her in the outskirts of the city, and supplied her with every comfort she could desire. He spent his holidays in her society. On these occasions he took her on little jaunts,* and attended to her dress and winter stores. When absent from her he wrote a long letter every week, in which he gave, just as he had given when he was a lad, an account of the sermons he had heard. He would willingly have taken her to London to keep house for him, but this she steadily refused. She was too old to learn London ways; she would have been an object of derision to some, a subject of gossip to others. Her ways were old-fashioned, her speech was broadly Scotch. She could never have managed servants. Only once did he prevail on her to come and see him. It was to visit the second Exhibition; but the confusion and noise were too much for her, and he did not press her to come again.

The last time I saw Bob was at his mother's funeral. He had become by that time a famous man in his art, and no one could have supposed, when they looked at the tall, fair-haired gentleman, who stood, with moist eyes, and uncovered, at the grave, or heard him speak his thanks to the company in the sweet English speech to which he had attained, that this was the same being who thirty years before had been a poor outcast boy seeking work in vain in the neighboring mills.

*Excursion, journeys, short trips

Review
Place II - III

1. Write down from memory as many things in this story that have to do with a law of health or a true remedy.

2. What was unhealthful about the place where Bob and his mother lived?

3. How did Bob's crime affect his own health? Did it affect anyone else?

4. How did a lack of **love** result in someone becoming a criminal?

5. If someone does not learn to **love** God, what might they **love** instead?

6. The 10 Commandments are a law of **love**. Which of them did Ned and Bob break?

7. If Ned could have found a way to get as much sweets as he liked honestly, would that have been all right?

8. How did Bob's sin affect his mother's health?

9. What was unhealthy about being in prison?

10. Why did Bob suffer more than Ned in prison?

11. How did Bob's body warn him to be careful with his feet?

12. What article of apparel was Bob too poor to own?

13. Who showed **love** to Bob while his mother was in the hospital? What did they do?

14. How did Bell's illness affect her work?

15. How did a loss of health result in a loss of work and therefore, the ability to buy food?

16. Bob saw the _____ between his crime and his mother's illness.

17. How did God show **love** for Bell and Bob?

18. Who showed **love** for the people of their community? How was their **love** shown practically?

19. How did the church members meet Bob?

Love • Love • Love • Love • Love • Love • Love • Love

20. How did a storekeeper in the story break a law of **love**?

21. How did people show **love** for Bob after he got his apprenticeship?

22. How did Bob show **love** for his mother when he became successful?

23. Although Bob changed in many things, there was no change in his ____ ____ ____ _____.

Designers in the 1800s

Read the Story, "Gertrude's Graveyard."

What Is Health? - Student - Page 80

Gertrude's Graveyard

Gertrude Murray was a decided enemy of tobacco. She used to say she hated it. Now hate is a strong, bad word, I know. My Mother has often said to me, "My dear, you should hate nothing but sin," and I never use the word but I think of my dear Mother and her advice. But I think, as Gertrude did, that it is quite proper to say "hate" in speaking of tobacco, for it is a terrible poison, and injures more persons, body and soul, too, than people are willing to believe.

But she did something besides hating it and calling it bad names. She tried to persuade everyone who used it to give it up. She was a strange child. She never acted like other children, but had a way all her own, which sometimes made folks cry and sometimes laugh, and always made them shake their heads, and say, "What a strange child Gertrude Murray is!"

She took a notion into her head one day that she would have a little graveyard all her own. There was quite a large piece of ground in the old garden behind the house where nothing was planted. There was a long row of blackberry bushes which hid this corner from the house windows, and she often used to go down there to play alone. It was one day after she had been to visit James True, the village undertaker, that she got the idea of having the graveyard. She went straight off to the woods and brought home four pretty little hackmatack trees, which she planted in the four-corners of the lot she had chosen, and then, happening to think it would be better to secure the ground by asking her father to give it to her, she went in pursuit of him.

"Papa! Papa!" she called aloud, as he was threshing grain in the barn.

"Papa, will you give me the north-west corner of the garden?"

"The what, child?"

"The north-west corner of the old garden, Papa. It is bounded on the north by the seek-no-further apple-tree, east by the walk, south

What is Health? - Student - Page 81

by the blackberry bushes, and west by the field of sweet corn."

There was a general laugh over this speech. Father and all the threshers stopped their work, and held their sides, while such peals of laughter resounded through the great barn as brought Mamma and Hepsty out to see what was the matter.

"You need not make fun of me," exclaimed Gertie; "I tried to be particular, just to save you the trouble of going down."

"Gertie wants me to deed her the north-west corner of the garden, Mother," said Mr. Murray as soon as he could speak; "are you ready to sign the papers?"

"What do you want it for, dear?" asked her Mother; "are you going to build a dollhouse?"

Her Mother knew that particular spot was her little girl's favorite resort, and that scarcely a day passed but the dollies were taken there, too. So she thought, of course, that Gertrude was planning some sort of a dwelling for them. She was quite unprepared for the answer, and the roar of laughter, which was repeated as the child looked up very meekly and replied, "I want it for a graveyard, Mamma."

When her father had recovered the power of speech, he pursued his inquiries further.

"What are you going to bury, dear?"

Quick as a flash of light, Gertrude picked up her father's pipe which lay on the wooden bench by the door. "This first," said she, and off she ran. So quick was her motion and the words that accompanied it, that no one of the amused group perceived what she had done; and as she flitted down the garden walk, they thought that she was only running from their mirth. But when the work was done and the farmer was ready for his evening smoke, the pipe was nowhere to be found.

"Where's my pipe? Who's seen my pipe?" shouted Father, up and down the yard, in no very pleasant tones.

"I buried it Papa, in my new graveyard," said the child coolly. "Come and see." The heavy steps of the tired man and the light trip-trip of the child's feet fell on the garden walk, as they proceeded to the north-west corner of the garden, where Gertrude pointed to a neat little mound about a foot long, nicely rounded and turfed, at the head of which was placed a bit of shingle with the inscription,—

HERE LIES
MY FATHER'S PIPE.
REST FOREVER.

The astonished parent was at a loss what to say. He hesitated whether to laugh or chide. He finally concluded to do neither, but to try to get at the child's meaning in all this. So, sitting down on an overturned wheelbarrow, he took Gertrude on his knees and began to question her.

"Why did you do so, child?"

"Because, Papa, I did not want you to die as Mr. Thurston did, of pipe. It is a fact, Papa," seeing a smile gathering in his eye. "I heard Dr. Small say so when we were coming home from the funeral. Miss Simpson asked him what ailed Mr. Thurston, and Dr. Small said, 'Pipe, Miss Simpson, pipe. He smoked himself out of this world. If folks get so used to their pipes in this world, I don't see what they are going to do in the other. Seems to me they will want to keep up smoking, but I'm most sure they can't do it in Heaven; for you know, Miss Simpson, Heaven is a clean place, and they are not going to let anything in there that defileth. So I don't know.' Now, Papa, you see I want you to be my Papa a long, long while first before you die, and then I want you to go to Heaven. So you see, I thought I would dig a grave and bury the old pipe. You won't dig it up, will you, Papa?"

The farmer held his peace for a few moments. Then he spoke slowly, but firmly:—

"No Gertie, your father is no grave robber. I shall miss the old pipe, I suppose; but I must say about it as we do about everything that's put in the grave. *'Thy will be done.'*"

"That's good, Papa," said the child with a kiss. "Now I have a good, clean, everlasting Papa. Isn't everlasting what we call things that don't die?" she added again, perceiving a smile.

What is Health? - Student - Page 83

"Yes, dear, but then none of us are everlasting, exactly; we all have got to wither and die sometime."

"Why, yes, Papa; but doesn't the Bible say that someday we can live forever?"

"Was that what you wanted this graveyard for?" asked the father smiling again, and seeking to divert the conversation, which he feared might get beyond his depth, "was it only to bury that old pipe?"

"No, indeed." exclaimed Gertrude earnestly, "I'm going to bury lots of such things here. I expect I shall have a funeral almost every day. I'm going to bury old Aunt True's snuff-box next."

"How will you get it?"

"Oh, I'll get it; I'll manage, Papa, and then there's Joe's tobacco, and Uncle Henry's cigar, and lots more of the nasty things."

Gertrude proved a busy little undertaker, and before a week had passed more than a dozen interments had been made in the new cemetery. The graves were all made evenly, side by side, exactly the same size, nicely rounded and turfed, and at the head of each a tiny board, on which was printed, with pen and ink, some simple epitaph. These head-boards cost the little girl a good deal of time and labor. On one was "Aunty True's snuff-box. Closed forever." On another, "Joe Tanner's pigtail. Lost to view." On the next, "Cyrus Ball's cigar. Burned out." All were equally characteristic.

The north-west corner lot was at length full. Over sixty neat little graves were there in rows as regular as the children's graves in Greenwood. The seek-no-further spread a friendly shade over the spot, and the blackberries ripened beside them; and many a visitor was taken slyly down the garden walk to see Gertie's graveyard. But the very best part of the whole was that for every little mound in that quiet spot there stood a man or woman redeemed from an evil habit, a living monument above it; and all alike bearing testimony to the faithfulness and perseverance of that strange little girl, the hater of tobacco, the **lover** of purity and health.

Mark Your Bible
Health

1. Does God care about our health?

III John 2 – *"Beloved, I wish above all things that thou mayest prosper and be in health, even as thy soul prospereth."*

2. Has eating and drinking anything to do with our religion?

I Corinthians 10:31 – *"Whether therefore ye eat, or drink or whatsoever ye do, do all to the glory of God."*

3. How much of a person is affected by Bible religion?

I Thessalonians 5:23 – *"And the very God of peace sanctify you wholly; and I pray God your whole spirit and soul and body be preserved blameless unto the coming of our Lord Jesus Christ."*

I Corinthians 6:19-20 – *"What? know ye not that your body is the temple of the Holy Ghost which is in you, which ye have of God, and ye are not your own?*

"For ye are bought with a price: therefore glority God in your body, and in your spirit, which are God's."

4. What is an important part of recovering from sickness?

Isaiah 1:16-17 – *"Cease to do evil; Learn to do well."*

5. When we stop breaking the laws of health, what is God able to do for us?

Psalm 103:1, 3 – *"Bless the Lord, O my soul: and all that is within me, bless his holy name. Who forgiveth all thine iniquities; who healeth all thy diseases."*

6. Christ bore our sickness as well as our sins.

Matthew 8:16-17 – *"When the even was come, they brought unto him many that were possessed with devils: and he cast out the spirits with his word, and healed all that were sick: That it might be fulfilled which was spoken by*

What is Health? - Student - Page 85

Esaias the prophet, saying, Himself took our infirmities, and bare our sicknesses."

7. What price did Christ pay that we might be healed?

Isaiah 53:5 – *"But he was wounded for our transgressions, he was bruised for our iniquities: the chastisement of our peace was upon him; and with his stripes we are healed."*

8. What are we promised if we obey all of God's laws?

Exodus 15:26 – *"If thou wilt diligently hearken to the voice of the Lord thy God, and wilt do that which is right in his sight, and wilt give ear to his commandments, and keep all his statutes, I will put none of these diseases upon thee, which I have brought upon the Egyptians: for I am the Lord that healeth thee."*

Health is Wealth!

What is Health? - Student - Page 86

At First I Prayed for Light

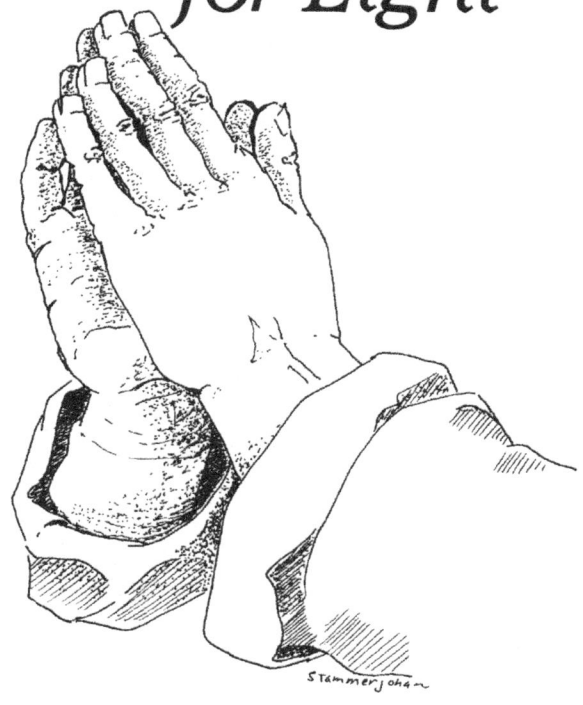

At first I prayed for light: Could I but see the way,
How gladly, swiftly would I walk to everlasting day!

And next I prayed for strength: That I might tread the road
With firm, unflattering feet, and win The heaven's serene abode.

And then I asked for faith: Could I but trust my God,
I'd live infolded in His peace, Though foes were all abroad.

But now I pray for **love**: Deep **love** to God and man;
A living **love** that will not fail, However Dark His plan.

And light and strength and faith Are opening everywhere!
God waited patiently until I prayed the larger prayer.

–Mrs. E.D. Cheney

Outline of School Program

Age	Grade	Program
Birth through Age 7	Babies Kindergarten and Pre-school	*Family Bible Lessons* (This includes: Bible, Science–Nature, and Character)
Age 8	First Grade	*Family Bible Lessons* (This includes: Bible, Science–Nature, and Character) + Language Program (*Writing and Spelling Road to Reading and Thinking* [WSRRT])
Age 9-14 or 15	Second through Eighth Grade	*The Desire of all Nations* (This includes: Health, Mathematics, Music, Science–Nature, History/Geography/Prophecy, Language, and Voice–Speech) + Continue using WSRRT
Ages 15 or 16-19	Ninth through Twelfth Grade	9 – *Cross and Its Shadow I** + Appropriate Academic Books 10 – *Cross and Its Shadow II** + Appropriate Academic Books 11 – *Daniel the Prophet** + Appropriate Academic Books 12 – *The Seer of Patmos** (Revelation) + Appropriate Academic Books *or you could continue using *The Desire of Ages*
Ages 20-25	College	Apprenticeship

Made in the USA
Monee, IL
21 August 2022